For Your Ears Only

For Your Ears Only

Nikki van der Zyl

IndePenPress

First published in Great Britain by Indepenpress

All paper used in the printing of this book has been made from wood grown in managed, sustainable forests.

ISBN13: 978-1-78003-451-5

Printed and bound in the UK

Indepenpress Publishing Limited
25 Eastern Place
Brighton
BN2 1GJ

A catalogue record of this book is available from the British Library

Cover design by Jacqueline Abromeit

I dedicate this book to the memory of my parents, to my husband George for his invaluable help and my daughter Kerry for her support.

CONTENTS

FOREWORD

BY NORMAN WANSTALL, SUPERVISING SOUND EDITOR

Nikki van der Zyl's contribution to the early James Bond movies is legendary. Her revoicing of many of the principal (and smaller part) actresses was demanding in the extreme and her professionalism was admired by all who worked with her.

Only rarely in film production are the voices of actors deemed to be unsuitable in terms of clarity, diction or accent, but throughout the early days of the Bond series actresses were cast for their visual suitability rather than their mastery of the English language. As a consequence the voices of several 'Bond Girls' were judged to have insufficient clarity for world markets and Nikki was selected for the highly specialised task of revoicing them.

Film actors are frequently required to re-record lines of their dialogue after a film is shot, especially if ambient conditions on location have made the original sound quality unacceptable. It's a straightforward procedure as actors are familiar with their own style of delivery and they rapidly recapture their original performance and timing. On the other hand, the task of replacing the voice of another actor and achieving perfect synchronisation, clarity and accent is a far greater challenge and only a specialised performer of Nikki van der Zyl's standing would be considered to take it on.

It is to Nikki's credit that her performances have never been questioned and her greatest reward is to witness the disbelief of those informed that Ursula Andress' voice is not her own. The same can be said of the voice of Claudine Auger in *Thunderball* and many others too numerous to name.

As is shown by the credits at the end of any movie, filmmaking is teamwork and in the case of those early Bond blockbusters Nikki played her part with distinction.

It is of great surprise to those who worked with Nikki that her name was never included in the credits.

CHAPTER 1
BERLIN BABY

Here's a paradox: countless millions of movie-goers and television viewers have heard my voice, but they have never heard of me!

In the first Bond film *Dr. No,* do you remember the beautiful Ursula Andress as Honey Ryder emerging from the sea singing 'Underneath the Mango Tree'? Do you remember the seductive voice she has throughout the film? Do you also remember Domino Derval in *Thunderball*, played by the beautiful leading actress Claudine Auger, or Raquel Welch in *A Million Years BC*? What about the gold-painted beauty played by Shirley Eaton in *Goldfinger*? The voice you heard coming from their mouths, throughout these films, is mine.

People always ask why Ursula had to be revoiced for *Dr. No* and I always reply that the producers had their reasons. She had a strong Swiss-German accent and I was told that her voice was not exotic enough. Ironically, I too had a strong German accent until I was nine years old, but more on that later.

After I revoiced Ursula Andress in *Dr. No*, I also did the same for many other female characters in the film. I revoiced Eunice Gayson both in *Dr. No* and again when she appeared in *From Russia With Love*. Her voice was deemed too posh for the character.

The first feature film I revoiced was *The Tale of Two Cities* in 1958. I spoke for the girl who was in the cell with Dirk Bogarde and who subsequently was in the cart with him as they were going to their execution. In 1960, I was engaged to revoice the actress Shirley Ann Field in *Man In The Moon* starring Kenneth More, and soon after that I revoiced Claudia Cardinale in *Lafayette*.

The film business is full of little tricks that few outsiders were privy to. I was never credited and there was never any publicity to divulge that the voices emanating from the many famous actresses were all mine. Indeed,

EON Productions, the company behind the Bond films, had no wish for the greater public to know that their stars did not speak for themselves. There was one critic who, when reviewing *Dr. No*, wrote 'Andress... has a voice that would sound sexy reading the telephone directory'. Another critic said she 'has a continental accent that can infuse even a comment on the weather with delicious mystery'. I felt so frustrated that I was tempted at that time to reveal that the voice was mine.

I am listed in *The Guinness Book of Movie Facts & Feats* as one of the most prolific actors and actresses who were never credited for their voice-over work. Consider Dave Prowse who played the imposing Darth Vader in *Star Wars*. Did you hear his friendly West Country accent emanating from inside his costume? No, of course not - that would not have lent much conviction to the fearsome character of Lord Vader. What you hear instead is the sonorous voice of black American actor James Earl Jones. Much more believable! It happens a lot in film, but unless you are told about revoicing (or dubbing as it is often wrongly called) you may never realise you have been hoodwinked - all in the name of art.

I was a trained actress who always wanted a part in the Bond films. After I revoiced Ursula Andress I was told that I would appear in the next film, but perhaps I was too useful doing the voices, for the onscreen roles never materialised. However, you will read more about my part in the Bond movies and other feature films series as my story unfolds.

But firstly, how did one unknown actress (me!) come to be recording her voice in the sound studios at Pinewood for another unknown actress at the time? Ursula Andress would become world famous for her role as Honey Ryder in *Dr. No*, the first James Bond film, but me …?

* * * *

The story starts when I was a child. I must have been around 11 years of age. My parents were called one day by the producers of a children's film which had been made in Germany. They had the German soundtrack but wanted it translated and dubbed into English. They had heard that I spoke German and wanted me to revoice the part of a little girl.

My mother came with me to Denham Studios, where the voicing was to take place and I spent the day there working on the film. By the end of filming, I knew I wanted to be an actress.

I spoke German because I was born in Berlin in 1935 – not the best place or time to be born into my Jewish family. The Nazis had come to power and Jews were certainly not the most popular people with the Nazi regime.

I remember a few things from my childhood at that time, which had nothing to do with being Jewish but were just the memories of a young child. For example, I was very small and when I looked up from my pram, all I could see were flashes of wheels and sides of cars going by very quickly. I could not see a driver, so I wondered what could make these machines move by themselves.

I also remember my father taking photos of me at the Berlin Zoo with my arm around a lamb. The photo was displayed in the window of a photographer's shop and my parents saw it one day as they were passing. Ironically, I looked like one of Hitler's ideal Aryan children, with my curly straw blonde hair and big blue eyes. I'm sure the photographer had no idea I was Jewish or else I doubt he would have put the large photo up on display in his shop front. Dad also took pictures of me taking my first steps in our local park in Prenzlauer Berg which, after the Second World War, became part of Communist East Berlin.

My mother and I fled our home in Berlin in 1939. My father had already left Berlin for London, having been rescued from the Nazis by the intervention of the Honourable Lily Montagu. She was influential and able to help my father because of her own standing as a pioneer woman in the Reform Jewish community and being one of ten children from the prominent Montagu Samuel family.

My father was a rabbi who served two congregations. He was young, good looking, had blond hair and was clean-shaven, with bright blue eyes that seemed to see right into you. He was charismatic and many women in his congregations fell in love with him from afar.

He was born in Schwerte, Westfalen in Germany on 11th September 1902, the son of Magnus van der Zyl and Lisette née Scheier. He received his teacher diploma in Munster and wrote his doctoral thesis in Giessen, Westfalia, where he graduated in 1931. He taught philanthropy in Frankfurt am Main and attended the Hochschule für die Wissenschaft des Judentums in Berlin, where his teacher was the renowned Rabbi Dr Leo Baeck.

In 1931 he married my mother, Anneliese Less and after graduation, was ordained a rabbi in Berlin.

He became the rabbi of the Friedenstempel and then the Neue Synagogue, Oranienburgerstrasse in Berlin, which is now a cultural centre and museum. Dad gave his last sermon there on 17th February 1938 and, as my mother told me, it was a service in commemoration of those who had died in the First World War. Dad's own father had fought for Germany in the First World War, so for him it was personal as well.

Ernst Bloch's *Sacred Service* was given its first performance on this occasion. Surrounded by the Jewish veterans who had been awarded the Iron Cross for bravery in the war, Dad said: "At that time we were celebrated for our heroism in the service of this country. Now we are criminals." The Gestapo were standing at the back of the synagogue and Dad knew this. My mother thought he would be arrested any minute and turned white. She has written an account of what happened then and I can do no better than to quote her. She wrote:

> Although there was no longer any hope for the survival of Jewish worship or activity, Werner [my dad] wanted to remain with his community, as did his teacher, Rabbi Dr Leo Baeck. Both of them were summoned before the Gestapo to be warned that if news of any actions against the Jews was published in any English newspaper, they would be held responsible.

To continue paraphrasing my mother's story, she said that shortly after this, Dad's parents told him that his brother had been arrested in Hanover. Dad immediately went there to help. At the same time, my parents were ordered to leave their home so Mum took refuge with her uncle in Berlin. He was Dutch and foreign citizens, even of the Jewish faith, were still safe there at that time. Later, Dad failed to return from Hanover and Mum had no news of him, so she went to Hanover to see what had happened. At the police station she innocently asked if they could find out from local hospitals if there had been an accident, as he had not returned.

Opposite the police station there was a prison, but she was coolly informed by the police officer that her husband was in a concentration camp. She took a taxi, frantic and crying, to Dad's parents. The taxi driver asked her if she was unwell and she replied "No, just Jewish." If the taxi driver had had a mind to report her, she would have been arrested immediately as she was not wearing her Star of David, which was compulsory for all Jews when out on the streets.

My mother was a beautiful woman. She was dark haired and blue-eyed. She was a tremendously talented pianist and would have made a name for herself as a concert pianist had Adolf Hitler not intervened in world affairs. As it was, she never got over the nervousness that engulfed her when she was forced to leave her homeland. As I said, I was a typical looking Aryan child and none of us looked Jewish, which is why Mum and I could walk through the streets of Hanover without the identifying Star of David. Nobody thought we were Jewish.

In the meantime, the wives of Dad's colleagues had received letters giving the whereabouts and signatures of their husbands in detention. Mum heard nothing and naturally feared the worst.

Three weeks later she received a letter from Dad. He was in the prison opposite the police station that Mum had visited. He was being kept in a darkened cell. Mum contacted the Hon. Lily Montagu in London. Miss Montagu knew Dad through his work for the World Union for Progressive Judaism in England. Her secretary spoke German and Mum told her that if Miss Montagu could procure a visa stating that Dad could find work in England and send it to the prison in Hanover, it was possible that he might be released.

While Dad was in prison he was being transferred from one floor to another by the prison warder. Dad thought he was being harassed, but the warder was, in fact, saving his life. The system worked like this: when a new person arrived, they were put on the ground floor and gradually they were moved up stairs. When they reached the top floor, they were transported to the concentration camps.

When Dad was ordered to appear before the Gestapo, he thought his last hour had come. The Gestapo liked to play deadly games. They asked him where he would go if he were free. He couldn't have known that Miss Montagu had procured a visa for him to go to England, so luckily for him he named England. Dad heard afterwards that if he had said the United States, he would not have been released. These were the unholy sports that amused the Gestapo mentality. Dad was then informed that he was free to go, but unless he left Germany within three weeks, he would be taken back into detention. Lily Montagu had done sterling work in rescuing my father.

Although he was free again, he still wanted to stay with his community. It was Leo Baeck who persuaded him to accompany a Kindertransport (the evacuation of children fleeing the Nazi regime) to England. This he did and after arriving in England, he realised the worsening situation, especially following the invasion of Czechoslovakia in March 1939. In England, the newspapers were full of reports of the conflict which was about to engulf Europe, plus accounts of what was happening in Germany specifically to the Jews. In Berlin, however, we were left in the dark and were ignorant of the larger picture. Dad telephoned Mum from London and told her to leave everything and come immediately with me to England. He was sending the necessary papers.

Mum's parents could not be persuaded to leave. They could not believe that their beloved Germany would ever harm them, just because they were Jews.

* * * *

I digress a little here to give a bit of background to my mother's family history.

Mother's great grandfather was a rabbi, but I don't have many details about him. He and his wife fathered Joel and Hermann Struck. Martha Struck, my grandmother, was the daughter of Joel and Joel's wife, Helena, who died in 1930. Martha Struck (1884-1942) married Leo Less (1887-1942) in Breslau where the Struck family lived, but Leo Less lived in Berlin. They moved there after they married and my mother was born in Weissensee in 1909. After mother married my father in Berlin, they moved to Pieskower Weg in Prenzlauer Berg, not far from Mum's parents.

So my maternal grandmother, Martha Struck, having married Leo Less, settled down in Weissensee at 18 Albertine Strasse, near the park. They opened a large men and boys' store in Weissensee, with apartment houses surrounding the large yard behind the shop in what would later become East Berlin. Many years after the war, Mr Patrick Stottrop bought the whole property and turned the store into a branch of his chain of ladies' fashion houses. The price he offered for it was generous at the time. Even when the economic climate became disadvantageous for him, he still honoured the agreement. A very nice and decent man, with whom I am still friendly.

Martha Struck's uncle, Hermann Struck (1876-1944), was a well-known artist and etcher. His book *The Art of Etching* became a leading work on the subject and his students included famed artists Marc Chagall and Max Liebermann. Hermann Struck was commissioned to create portraits of such figures as Albert Einstein, Henrik Ibsen, Friedrich Nietzsche, Sigmund Freud, Theodor Herzl, Oscar Wilde and other foremost figures of the time. Struck and Liebermann remained lifelong friends and there is much more about them on the Internet for the interested reader.

* * * *

But back to the story; my mum and I were on the Berlin Hauptbahnhof (main railway station) platform, having to leave Mum's parents there, waiting for the train to take us to the airport, from where we would fly from Germany to England and start a new life.

Mum said goodbye to her parents and I can still see the scene. I cried out 'Omi' and 'Opa' as I said goodbye to Grandma and Grandpa. Tears streamed down Mum's face as she knew we would never see them again. We never did.

Grandpa suffered a heart attack before he could be taken off to a concentration camp and Grandma was murdered by the Nazis in Theresienstadt concentration camp.

The journey to England was one I still remember, even though I was only four years old at the time. The noise of the plane engines and the pain in my ears remain vivid in my memory. During the flight, Mum was in a really bad state, understandably so, and later she told me that I had said to her in German, "Mummy don't upset yourself so much." This coming from a four-year-old must have impressed her.

The plane was scheduled to land in Holland where my mother (as I understand it now) had to get a valid pass for me. She was told I could not land in the UK without one. Mum took the opportunity to see her best friend, Lutzi and her husband, who had taken refuge there. It was all extremely traumatic and delayed our journey by a couple of days. Dad was going frantic as he did not know what was going on and could only imagine that all manner of dreadful things had befallen us.

My mother's German passport, emblazoned with swastikas and a large red 'J' for Jude (Jew), contained a stamped visa issued by the UK consular service in Berlin. It stated that she must register with the police and not remain in the UK for longer than six months. It also stated boldly 'GOOD FOR SINGLE JOURNEY ONLY'. How reassuring!

Mum and Dad in the year of their marriage, 1931

Berlin baby

At the Berlin Zoo

Cute and curly

Clinging to Mum before fleeing the Nazis

CHAPTER 2
NEW BEGINNINGS AS A REFUGEE

We landed at Croydon Airport on Mum's thirtieth birthday – 27th March 1939.

That is how I came to be in England and why I spoke German. It was, after all, my first language.

Many of the earlier recollections are based on what my mother wrote in the book entitled *Werner van der Zyl Master Builder*, which was published by the Reform Synagogues of Great Britain in 1994, as a tribute to my father on the 10th anniversary of his death.

After staying for a while with Ernest Joseph, an architect who lived in North London, we went on to a hotel in Finchley Road, London. We (Mum, Dad and I) then found ourselves in a house in Coverdale Road in Cricklewood. All our belongings, which had been packed into a container in Berlin before we left, never arrived. This included all my toys, our clothes and other personal items. As we had no money we could not replace anything.

War between Britain and Germany was declared in September 1939. Dad had a strong sense of duty and gratitude to have been taken in by England as a German Jewish refugee. He became a volunteer firefighter. He went out every night to help with the fires that started when the Germans dropped their lethal bombs. One night our whole road was bombed. The noise of houses collapsing sent Dad rushing back home. He must have thought we were both dead. Our house was the only one left standing, but it was damaged and unsafe. When Mum came into my bedroom to see if I was alright, I asked her if the wardrobe had fallen over. I knew something bad had happened to our house, but wanted to make light of it. We had to leave very quickly and it is all a bit hazy now, but I remember being taken to the countryside near Ramsgate. Being bombed out of our home made us feel at one with our English compatriots! I had developed whooping cough so Mum came with me to Ramsgate, while Dad stayed in London.

Dad's daytime work was with refugee children who had arrived in England because of the war and who had been separated from their parents. He directed their placement and education from the offices in Bloomsbury House, the wartime headquarters of the Central British Fund, which overnight became the one sure address for Jewish refugees.

After a while, Mum and I returned to London where Dad rented a flat in Buckland Crescent, Swiss Cottage. It was on the ground floor of a big house which had been converted into flats. We had large rooms; a lounge which doubled as a bedroom for my parents and one other room which was my bedroom. Mum had her beloved piano in the lounge and we ate there as the room looked onto the garden from the patio windows. From there I attended a primary school in Kilburn.

It was not easy starting a new life in a new country speaking a foreign language and I made some mistakes. I thought I had to go to school on Saturdays as well as weekdays. I don't know why I was under that impression but put it down to not understanding English properly. I told my parents I had to go to school on Saturday mornings. This was a difficult situation as it is the Jewish Sabbath and my father officiated at services. We got to Kilburn the first Saturday morning and the school gates were closed. I was told off about my mistake.

But I do remember the sweet shop across the road and buying some boiled sweets with some of the boys and girls from the school.

Speaking of not understanding the language, my father told me a story about his lack of English in those early days. He went into a shop and asked for a cake. When told the price, he exclaimed: "Oh, but I can get a cheaper tart round the corner."

Mum's English was also not very good yet. One day we all got on a double-decker bus and Dad went upstairs while she stayed with me on the lower deck. The conductor came to get the fares and Mum tried to explain that Dad would be paying. The German word *Herr* usually translates as *mister* but can also mean *Lord*. Mum unwittingly caused some amusement by saying to the conductor, "That's all right, the Lord above will pay."

There were many such funny occasions, but we tried to adjust to English life as quickly as possible.

During the night-time air raids, Mum would put me in a green siren suit with a hood and we would walk to Swiss Cottage Station. It seemed a long walk to me then and quite frightening, as no street lights were allowed to be on and it was difficult to see one's way. We would finally get to the station and join a crowd of people with the same idea of being safe from the bombs. The atmosphere was good natured and friendly and we felt protected. One night we took a torch to help find our way there and a policeman was instantly at our side telling us to turn it off. We never took a torch again.

Occasionally, if we didn't want to walk to the station during a raid, we would crouch under the dining room table thinking that it might protect our heads if a bomb fell on the roof. Ironically, soon after the war ended, our lounge ceiling collapsed onto the table, splitting it in half. So much for its protection!

In 1941, when I was six years old, with the bombings continuing, my parents felt that it was not safe for me to stay in London any longer. They managed to get a place for me in a school called Stoatley Rough in Haslemere, Surrey. There were many refugee children there and the school was set in a beautiful location.

My mother took me to the school, which seemed a huge place to me. It was at the top of a steep hill at the bottom of which was a farm, where cows, sheep and horses were kept. I decided to explore while Mum was talking to the headmistress.

I remember falling down and hurting myself. My first instinct was to cry, but then I thought about it. There was nobody around and I was on my own. I might just as well get up as no one was going to help me. It was a turning point for me as, from then on, I realised I would just have to rely on myself. It would be a case of sink or swim and I had no intention of sinking.

I was six and had never been parted from my parents before. Now I was on my own and realised that the world was a hard place. I became a rebel. I resented not having my parents with me and turned into a very naughty child. I got into fights with the boys, climbed trees and generally behaved wildly. I still have the scar from one occasion when, out of curiosity, I opened another child's tuck box. I broke a glass and in the process cut my left thumb quite badly.

Many years later I was told by my friend Susi Weissrock, who had been at school with me, that I was the leader of a gang – something I was totally unaware of at the time! She said that when new pupils arrived they were asked which gang they wanted to join, Attulah's or mine. I do remember seeing my friend walking up the hill one hot day in the summer and asking her what she was doing. Susi said she had to get Atullah a glass of water. I was outraged and said Attulah should get it herself. The difference apparently was that Attulah used her gang as slaves to fetch and carry, whilst I looked after and protected my gang from Attulah. Apparently, I had more members, although to this day I cannot remember ever having had a gang at all.

Susi's family knew my parents from Germany and they were very fond of them, so there was a strong connection with them all. Susi had two sisters at Stoatley Rough, Helga and Ruth, who were older than us, but the eldest sister, Gaby, had left school by then. Helga and Ruth helped look after us younger ones. I was lonely and missed my parents. I found it hard to get to sleep at night. I remembered my mother gently stroking my arms at home before I fell asleep, so I thought it would be nice if Helga could do that for me. I offered her a penny to do it, but I don't think she ever took the proffered penny. She did stroke my arms and that did help me to sleep. Later in my life, George (my second husband) took over and gently caresses me by stroking my face and hair, which calms me and quickly puts me to sleep, either in bed or on the couch, especially if we're watching a boring programme on TV. But I'm jumping ahead here.

The headmistress, Dr Lion (pronounced in the German manner as *Lee-on*), was an outstanding woman who had fled Germany herself and was deeply involved in education. She was a remarkable innovator. It was only years later that I appreciated what she did.

At the time, I got into much mischief because of my pranks, at least one of which was at her expense. She had a strong German accent and had a habit of saying 'hem, hem' at the end of every sentence. It sounded like a snort and one day I decided to bring a large sow up from the farm. I led her to a spot in front of Dr Lion's bungalow and she started to snort. I had brought half my class out to watch what would happen. Dr Lion came out and was most indignant, but after each outburst she said 'hem, hem'. She sounded the same as the pig and we were all in stitches.

I was always being accused of talking in class, sometimes falsely. I got exceedingly angry with one teacher called Miss Gretz, who was always picking on me. I was a small child and could get into small openings. One day, to have my revenge, I crouched under her chair and shouted out that Miss Gretz had pink knickers on. The class loved it and giggled. She went bright red and complained to the head.

Another time the whole school went down with mumps and I caught it too. I was in the infirmary and at the end of my bed two teachers were discussing me, speaking in German. They obviously didn't know I could understand what they were saying, but the gist of it was that I was faking mumps to get out of classes. I had a painful and swollen neck and told them in German, and in no uncertain terms, that I really was ill! They got quite a shock.

On Christmas Eve all the children were given Christmas stockings to put up so that Santa could put presents in them. I vividly remember feeling incredibly guilty about putting mine up, as a Jewish child, but was consoled by the thought that Father Christmas would know I was Jewish and would merely pass by my stocking without filling it. The next morning I woke up and to my horror (and guilty excitement) I found the stocking was full.

There was a wonderful man at Stoatley Rough who was the gardener. He used to take me round the allotments and show me the many vegetables he was growing and the flowers. There were not many of the latter because growing food was more important during the war, but I loved the colours and smells of the flowers. He used to let me sample the tomatoes he grew and I can still taste them in my mind, so fresh and sweet. One day I went round to the allotments, as I usually did, to find him. He was not in the allotments, nor in the shed and I couldn't understand why he was nowhere to be found. I walked in to the dining room and asked loudly if anyone knew where he was. One girl got up and came over to me and said he had died. I asked her what 'died' meant and she said I would never be able to see him again as he had gone to heaven. I was heartbroken. He was the nearest thing to an uncle that I had at the school.

We pupils at Stoatley Rough were almost always hungry. Meals were sparse and I remember we had one tiny square of butter that had to last us for a whole week. Food was at a premium. Susi and I once found a bag of potatoes round the back of the kitchen and proceeded to open the bag and eat the raw unpeeled potatoes to assuage our hunger. We didn't feel bad about it; sheer hunger made us devour those vegetables as if they were the most wonderful delicacy.

My father would occasionally come to the school in his capacity as a rabbi but that stopped when he was interned under the emergency Enemy Aliens Act, in 1940. My mother also visited sometimes, and occasionally I had been allowed to go back to London to be with them for the holidays, but when they were interned, I didn't see them at all.

As a consequence of their internment, Dad was sent to the Kitchener Camp in Richborough, Kent. As the spiritual leader and one of the administrators, he organised the educational and cultural activities there, but mostly he was the trusted rabbi who provided the affectionate and caring moral support needed. He propped up the many refugees, whose greatest need then, was for faith. In *Werner van der Zyl, Master Builder*, one of the chapters was written by Hans Francken, a fellow internee. He explains that Rabbi van der Zyl's role was to deal with many divergent groups: intellectuals, youngsters from the East End and people of different religions. Dad also had a social role. For example Francken quotes the case of a good-looking young man who was in danger of being seduced by an older man living in the same building in the camp. It is not revealed how my father resolved this situation, only that he had to deal with the many and varied problems that arose.

Women were not allowed to be with their husbands in the internment camps, but Mum, as the wife of the rabbi, was allowed to join him. There were many talented Jews there. Architects helped improve the living quarters, playwrights had their plays performed and Mum organised an orchestra. In the camp, all of this activity boosted morale and they gave concerts in the surrounding villages. Professor Norman Bentwich and his wife often allowed them to have musical evenings in their home in Deal and sometimes he would play the violin accompanied by Mum on the piano. He was a great support.

When the bulk of the refugees were transferred from Richborough to the Isle of Man they found the conditions there were worse, so Dad volunteered to go with them as camp rabbi.

He worked where he was most needed: with the men in internment camps and with more than 8,000 children scattered throughout hundreds of communities among thousands of Jewish and non-Jewish families.

* * * *

I was on my own in a boarding school in the countryside, but I was born and bred in the city and was very much a city girl. I missed London and the sights and smells of the town. When cars and lorries arrived, I smelt the petrol and a bit of London went up my nose as I breathed in the fumes. I did the same with the smell of tarmac, when the roads were being repaired.

Although being apart from my parents was nobody's fault, I still felt lonely and abandoned. This resulted in me doing many things that annoyed the teachers and I was continuously being complained about. The head liked me and didn't want to expel me, but the teaching staff were adamant that I had to go.

I still remember saying goodbye to Dr Lion. She had tears rolling down her cheeks. She was an affectionate lady and I was sorry that she was so upset. I felt very bad and guilty.

After leaving that school I was enrolled into the Clare Park School for Young Ladies in Farnham, Surrey. From the ridiculous to the sublime! I was certainly not a young lady but a tomboy who loved nothing more than to climb trees and mess about. I went from the frying pan into the fire.

There was a lot of misunderstanding in those days about German refugees who were themselves victims of the Nazis. Some people could not differentiate between them and the German enemy. They thought everyone with a German accent was the enemy, and because I still had an accent, I was treated quite badly.

My favourite pastime was to go on the nearby heath with the horses and enjoy the countryside. Although I was a city girl, I loved the gentleness of the countryside and drank in the colours of the flowers and trees against the sky. I also preferred being with horses rather than humans. But I also remember sitting under the trees and wishing I could go home and live with my parents.

Mum and Dad were released from the Isle of Man in 1943 and came back to their flat in Buckland Crescent, Swiss Cottage. My father accepted an invitation to become the rabbi of the North Western Reform Synagogue in Alyth Gardens, North London, (known commonly just as Alyth) and I came home to spend the Easter holidays with them. That was great as I had missed them so much.

It was unusual for me to come home for holidays while bombs were still falling, but this time it was for a specific reason. I thought it was because my birthday falls around Easter, but that was not the point of my returning to London that holiday.

I was then almost ten years old. From an early age I had squinted and worn a black patch over one eye. What I didn't know was that my father had arranged for me to have an operation at the Moorfields Eye Hospital. I was to be a guinea pig because that type of operation was in its infancy. My mother was worried as the surgeons had told my father there was a fifty-fifty chance of me either being cured or going blind. Mum's hair turned grey during that time. Thankfully, I was totally ignorant of the severity of the operation.

As I wrote earlier, I knew I wanted to become an actress. Though my English was improving, I was unable to pronounce my 'r's properly. I always said 'straight' with the rolling 'rrr' sound made at the back of the throat. This bothered me but endlessly amused my surgeon, who always asked me to say the word 'straight' at each of our meetings before my operation.

Just before I went to the operating theatre, someone came to cut my eyelashes, presumably to allow the surgeon to get as close to the eyeball as possible. On the day of the operation, I was administered gas and air with a mask held over my face. These were the days before anaesthesia would be injected via a needle. It was horrible. I quickly went under but had a nightmare and became conscious in the middle of the operation. They had given me too little gas and had to give me some more. I dreamt I was walking along a mustard-coloured beach with no end in sight. It was truly awful. I woke up to hear swear words coming from the surgeon which I had never heard before.

When I came back to the ward, I had bandages covering my eyes. It felt dreadful and I tried to peep out from under them, but I had to keep them on. My mother came to see me every day and I would guess what colour dress she was wearing. She brought me lilies-of-the-valley and their smell was divine. Since then I have always loved their scent. I was also taught how to knit in the hospital (through feel) by the ladies on the ward who were kind to me. I have since, as an adult, made up my own patterns and knitted stylish jumpers which I designed myself. Whenever I wear them, people ask me where I bought them and when I say I knitted them myself, they're impressed and ask if I can knit one for them too.

A week after the operation, I was looking forward to coming home. To my horror I was told the surgeon had to do the operation again, for my other eye. This scared me, although the second op wasn't as bad as the first. However, I had to keep the bandages over my eyes for three more weeks.

With the bandages on, it was like being blind and it seemed as though my hearing became incredibly acute. I realised that the accent I retained was because the 'rrr' sound I was making was being created at the back of my throat. I thought it could be cured by moving the sound to the front of my mouth. I practised it over and over again and finally managed to get it right.

I had my 10th birthday in hospital. My parents knew I wanted a scooter. I had seen my friends riding on their metal scooters and wanted to be like them and have one exactly the same as theirs. My parents had precious little money, but they brought a huge parcel into the hospital. I was very excited. It must be the scooter I had asked for! They had obviously spent a lot of money on giving me something I really wanted. They helped me remove the paper it was wrapped in, with my bandages still around my eyes. I felt the shape. It really was a scooter. Hurray... but then I touched it and realised it was made of wood! My heart sank, but I couldn't let them know I was disappointed. They must have thought this wooden one was better than the metal ones and it may well have been sturdier and a better buy, but I had been waiting for one just like my friends' scooters and now I had something completely different again. Oh dear! It was the first good acting job in real life I ever did.

I showed a happy face, kissed them and thanked them excitedly and they never knew I was disappointed with their thoughtful and expensive present.

After I was discharged from hospital, I returned to have my stitches out, which in itself was pretty horrendous, as I was given nothing to lessen the discomfort. My mother was beside herself knowing the pain I was experiencing. At last the ordeal was over.

This was the first visit to the hospital since my operation and the surgeon wanted to see me. Inevitably, he asked me to say 'straight'. Now there was no German sound to it at all. He was amazed and I think a little disappointed, but I was thrilled that I had succeeded in losing any trace of a German accent. Actresses on the screen didn't have foreign accents – not in my book! However, I did retain a legacy from the operations and that was bloodshot eyes. To this day, the whites of my eyes are still pink and my eyelashes have never grown long again.

It was extremely brave of my parents to make me undergo two operations and now I didn't have to wear a patch or spectacles. And as part of my desire to be English and fit in with my English friends, I had also lost my German accent.

I went back to school feeling far better. I now had no squint and I spoke like an English girl. I was a Clare Park Schoolgirl, even though I still yearned to go home for good to my parents in London. They had taken a gamble on my eyes and been through so much anxiety themselves. I had a lot to be grateful for.

Yet I still missed the city and even here at Clare Park, every time a vehicle arrived at the school gates, I again went to smell the petrol.

Eventually, in 1945 the war ended and I returned to my beloved London. I still remember the thrill of going to The Mall in London with Dad to celebrate Victory in Europe (VE) Day and to wait for the King and Queen, their princesses and Winston Churchill himself to come out onto the balcony of Buckingham Palace. The roar of the crowd was overwhelming. The relief of everyone that the war had ended in Europe was tangible. The anxiety of families with relatives serving in the forces was over, and the people who had lost loved ones and/or homes might now be able to start a new life. All this emotion, relief and pride in our victory and our country flowed from the crowd. We became one huge family who showed our love and gratitude to the Royal Family who had stayed in London and especially to the man with the courage to fight and give us confidence in that fight, Winston Churchill. The cheers could be heard for miles and went on for hours. Dad always admired Churchill and thought him the greatest leader in the world.

Trafalgar Square pigeons

Mum and me in London

CHAPTER 3
AN ENGLISH SCHOOLGIRL

I now found myself living in London with my parents for the first time in years, enjoying a normal family life. I could be a child again. I had roller skates and skated to the end of our road, which seemed endless at the time. Susi and her sisters lived round the corner from us and I used to go and see them on my skates. As a child it felt a very long way. Since then I have been back and the road doesn't seem long at all, of course. There was a bomb site across the road from our place and I went scrumping with Susi and other friends, picking apples from the former garden of the house which had been destroyed.

My father was busy with the synagogue at Alyth, but he still found time to take me for long walks. He knew about the trees and plants and told me their names. We talked about all sorts of things, including Jewish traditions and the afterlife. The strange thing was that he never told me what he personally believed. He used to say things like "some people believe this and others that…", never giving me his own ideas about the subjects we discussed. I think he was just unable to talk about his true feelings.

After the war our family life soon included my father's stepmother, Emma. She was the second wife of my paternal grandfather, Magnus van der Zyl and I called her 'Omi'.

* * * *

Just before the Second World War broke out, Omi had somehow got herself to Brussels and then hid from the Gestapo who patrolled the city's streets. She stayed there for the entire duration of the war and was never caught. After the conflict had ended, Dad asked the Red Cross to see if they could find her and they did. They brought her to us and we lived together happily for many more years. Omi couldn't speak English and she never did learn. I had been speaking nothing but English for years and had forgotten a lot of my German, so this was a good opportunity to relearn my native language. I became really fluent in German then. Omi was always good company and there for me when Mum and Dad went out.

My father's brother, Erich was not as lucky as Omi. He was discovered in Brussels by the Gestapo and sent back to Germany to die in a concentration camp.

Dad's younger brother, Kurt had left Germany earlier to go to Argentina with his wife and daughter, Renate. Dad had two other siblings, Harry and Bella, who had died in childhood. Later, Uncle Kurt's wife died and he remarried a friend of ours living nearby, who had also fled from Germany, Eva Reich. She joined Kurt in Argentina and they had a daughter called Veronica. Being so far away, we never got to meet Kurt's family until years later when Veronica once came to London with her husband. They were a lovely couple and I got on really well with this cousin and her husband. Such a shame we are so far apart. We do communicate by email, but it's not the same as being able to see each other.

So after the war, we were a family again – Omi, Mum, Dad and me. I did normal things for once, like going to a day school in Cricklewood and coming home after school on the tram. I was quite frightened of the tram as it made no noise when it approached and then suddenly it was there. This was all new to me and I revelled in being an ordinary schoolgirl. I took my eleven-plus examination to go on to secondary school, but either the teaching at Stoatley Rough and Clare Park was not good or I was a rotten pupil because I failed the test miserably. However, my father was determined that his daughter should have a decent education. He approached the headmistress of Paddington and Maida Vale High School, Miss Spong, and asked her if she would take me on. She made me sit an entrance examination, which apparently I passed with flying colours and so I was accepted. I joined the school in 1946 and some eventful moments followed.

* * * *

I was in the first form with a girl called Barbara Savage. One morning, we had just arrived at school and were hanging up our coats in the cloakroom when, out of the blue, she suddenly turned on me with some nasty remarks which included the fact that I was "horrible and Jewish". Up until then I had personally never encountered any overt anti-Semitism. I was gobsmacked, but I was a very physical girl and my first instinct was to hit her hard – so I followed my instinct and did just that! To my horror she fell back, seemingly lifeless and I was convinced that I had killed her. Our form teacher, Miss Genge was walking by so I rushed over to her and told her I thought I had killed Barbara. She went to examine the 'dead' Barbara, but all that had happened was that she had passed out after falling back and hitting her head on one of the coat hooks. She soon came round and I was relieved. But I never had any problems with her after that and Miss Genge left the cloakroom with a smile on her face.

I went through lots of schoolgirl crushes on female teachers. I admired Miss Genge, especially after she relieved me of the fear that I had murdered Barbara Savage. She was not only our form mistress but also our French teacher. We got on very well, even keeping up our friendship in our exchange of letters after she left the school to get married and live in Sweden. I started to learn Swedish then, so that if I ever went to see her in Gothenburg, I could make myself understood in that country.

Beryl Sellers was both our class teacher and our French teacher. I seem to have had a 'thing' for French teachers. We used to meet and go to school on the bus together and it became a pleasant platonic friendship. I used to go to her home where I met her mother who was a lovely lady.

One day Beryl met Edgar when he was in London on leave from his job in Hong Kong. They fell in love and, because he only had a short time before having to return, they decided to get married quickly. He was also a refugee from Germany who had to leave because of the Nazis. When Beryl first told me all this, I was upset that she was going so far away, but she said she would be coming home on leave in a year's time. A year! That's an age when you are young when a year feels like an interminably long time. Today, hundreds of moons later, I am complaining at how swiftly the years pass, but back then the weeks and years seemed to drag on forever. However, Beryl sweetened the pill by asking me to be her bridesmaid at her wedding. She and Edgar were to be married in the Methodist chapel near to where she lived. I told my father about me being a bridesmaid to Beryl, but because Edgar was Jewish and Beryl was not and they were getting married in church, Dad didn't allow me to be her bridesmaid. I was bitterly disappointed but our friendship endured, and after I was married and had my own children, Beryl used to come to see me when she was over here on leave from her post in Hong Kong. She was a teacher in one of the finest schools there.

Another teacher I liked was the French conversation teacher, Mademoiselle Claude Pavaut, a young woman from France. What was this thing about French teachers? We used to go for walks in the local park. She was in our school for only a year after which she went back to France.

Later, I went to a family who lived in Thionville, near Metz in France as an au pair. In those days it was the custom for French families to invite English pupils learning French to spend a week or so with them, to perfect their accent. The family was lovely and their daughter came to my family shortly after for the same purpose, to learn English.

While I was in France I phoned Mademoiselle Claude and she invited me to visit her in the home in Besançon she shared with her mother. We had a great time and one day, walking round her town, we held hands. She was extremely beautiful and I admired her greatly. I was thrilled she had held my hand and that night, after we had all gone to bed, I couldn't sleep. I was so excited. I decided to go to her room and crept along the corridor. My heart was pounding and I don't know what I expected to happen, but I went on anyway. She heard me come in and told me to come into her bed. I did so and she started stroking me. That was pleasurable, but then she suddenly kissed me on the lips and I had not expected that. I suppose I was very naïve, but it was all too much and I did not want that. Totally confused, I turned away and she apologised.

Next morning she apologised again and I had no idea how to react. I was utterly bewildered by what had happened. It was not her fault; I was the one who had come into her room. I did not think she was a lesbian, but just liked me a lot as I liked her.

It is quite difficult when the only way to show real affection is in a physical way. We stayed in touch a long time after that, so there were never any hard feelings on either side.

The female teachers always seemed to return my feelings, but by then I had also developed a healthy fondness for the boys I met at that time. So with hindsight I realise it was just a phase I was going through.

* * * *

I loved music which was encouraged by my parents. In the summer, when the Promenade Concerts were on I made my way to the Royal Albert Hall in Kensington and queued up for standing tickets. At the end of each concert I would wait for the conductor, Sir Malcolm Sargent to come out of the artiste's entrance. I wanted to stand out from the crowd who was waiting for him, so I used to climb up the layers of window sills above the artistes' stage door and call out to him. Eventually, after weeks of these antics, he started to look up for me. We started talking to each other and one day he gave me two tickets for the concert. My mother and I sat in the front row of the stalls. Afterwards we went round to his room and he was very kind. I sometimes went on my own too and because he was fond of me, he would kiss me on the cheek.

Whenever Sir Malcolm was recording in the Maida Vale Studios, as it was just around the corner from my school, he would invite me there and through him I met two other conductors, Sir Thomas Beecham and Sir Adrian Boult, a real treat.

I was often invited to Malcolm's flat across the road in Albert Mansions where I first met his butler, Oliver. He was kind to me and when I phoned Malcolm he always put me through to him. Malcolm had a lovely little budgerigar called Hughie and I used to talk to him as well.

He (Malcolm not Hughie) tried to kiss me on the lips one day and I shouted at him and he stopped. I wrote him a letter saying I was not about to let him make love to me. Besides, I was still a virgin. However, he was a household name and I suppose I was proud of knowing him and boasted a bit about it. When I was at school, I used to confide in Miss Spong, the headmistress and after one concert when I was excited about seeing Sir Malcolm, I told her that he had kissed me. This confidence came back to haunt me.

As a Jewish pupil, I was excused Religious Instruction (RI) lessons and so spent these lessons doing my homework in the library. One day, a fellow Jewish pupil in my class, Natalie Seymour, as she was then, came over to me and said that the teacher who was giving the RI lesson was making disparaging remarks about the Jews. I wanted to see for myself, so I attended the next RI lesson to hear what was being said.

The teacher was studying the Jewish Passover with the class, but all sorts of anti-Semitic myths were being introduced. I intervened and tried to put the true position diplomatically to her rather than punch her, as I had done to Barbara Savage. But the teacher started hurling books at me, then stormed out of the classroom. She went to see Miss Spong and I was called in later to tell her my side of the story.

She then said I was not to tell my father about the incident or else she would tell him that Sir Malcolm had kissed me. I was extremely upset about the whole business and after some soul-searching, decided, come hell or high water that I would tell my dad what had happened. After he heard the story, instead of being angry with me, he was furious with Miss Spong. He went to the school and demanded an explanation. It was not just the anti-Semitism, but the blackmail all rolled into one that my father and I could not abide. He told her that unless she sacked the RI teacher, he would take me out of school. (After all, I was sixteen and had already passed the O-Level exams, so it was legitimate to leave school then.) As the head decided to retain the RI teacher, my father removed me the next day. My friends later told me they could not understand why I had suddenly disappeared.

It was the first time that I personally had come across an adult with a blatant hatred for Jewish people and that startled me. I believed then, and still do, that all groups are made up of individuals and that it is the quality of a person that counts and not their colour or religion. I have never understood what makes anyone hate a whole race of people.

CHAPTER 4
ARTISTIC STIRRINGS AND INTERNAL PAINS

At that time one of my favourite cinema stars was the English actress Greer Garson. Before I left grammar school, Miss Garson herself had visited us and I enjoyed her fascinating lecture about her life and film career. I wanted to be up there on the screen with her.

It was during this time that I joined an amateur dramatic society called Lanercost Entertainment Society. It was started by a Jewish group and I took part in plays such as George Bernard Shaw's *Pygmalion* and Noel Coward's *Blithe Spirit*. I played Eliza in *Pygmalion* and Elvira in *Blythe Spirit*. Jerome Karet and Marcus Sefton-Green were also in the company. I revelled in being on stage in front of a live audience. Later, Jerome and Marcus were to join my father's synagogue in Alyth Gardens and with my father's love of young people, they became stalwarts of the North Western Reform Synagogue.

I was constantly surrounded by music. Mum played the piano as I did my school homework and she had taken me to concerts from an early age. The eminent pianist Myra Hess had given piano recitals at the National Gallery during the war and my mother had taken me to these concerts during my holidays in London. I was thrilled listening to Myra Hess and this increased my love of music already instilled in me by my parents.

Before the war and the Nazi regime, my mother had shown considerable talent as a pianist. Her teacher was a distinguished pianist himself. He told my grandmother that it would be terrible if Mum was not encouraged to become a professional pianist. My grandparents were old-fashioned and it was not considered 'seemly' for a nice Jewish girl to become a performer, however gifted. A shame as with my mother's personality and drive, she would have made it in Berlin. As it happened, tragically, the Nazis put an end to her potential career. By the time we had said goodbye to her parents and fled to England, her nerves were shattered. She was never able to play in public again. She sometimes played for the Ladies' Guild in the synagogue, but even then she was so nervous before the event, she had to be forced to enter the room. She was a fantastic pianist and continued playing right up until a couple of years before she died.

While I did my homework upstairs in my room, Mum played mostly Chopin pieces, such as the Fantasy Impromptu in C sharp minor and his preludes. She also loved playing Schubert and Bach. I once asked her what her favourite piano piece was and she said Chopin's F minor Fantasie. I felt fortunate to have such wonderful background music while I was working.

I also had inherited a love of music from my father's side. He had studied Jewish liturgy in order to become a cantor. He had a beautiful singing voice, but during his studies in Germany, he had also discovered a love of the Jewish religion and that is why he decided to become a rabbi. Of course, he was still able to sing in the services and he did this most effectively, especially in the Friday evening Sabbath services when he sang the Kiddush.

For a long time I had been having dreadful stomach pains. They were so bad that I couldn't sleep and Mum took me to our doctor who sent me to see various consultants. I had tests and X-rays galore yet nothing was found. My mother was told I was imagining the pains, or that perhaps they were simply growing pains. I knew none of this was true.

We finally ended up in the London University College Hospital. There I was seen by a group of students and one of them took down everything I said. When I had finished describing the intense pain I had most nights and exactly where the pain lodged, he said we should X-ray my gallbladder. His fellow students scoffed at him and said that he had 'gallbladder on the brain' as he was specialising in it. They said that it was the fair, fat and 40-year-olds who were the typical sufferers and I didn't fit that category at all. Although fair-haired, I was 16 and slim! This student retorted that I'd had every X-ray under the sun except for that one and he couldn't see the harm in another on my gallbladder, if only to eliminate that possibility. Lo and behold, it transpired I had 16 gall stones! He was right and he almost certainly saved my life. It was great to know at last that I was not imagining the pains, to know what it was and that it could be cured.

My father asked the prominent surgeon Arthur Dickson Wright, who was the surgeon to the royal household, to perform the operation. He did so and discovered that my gallbladder was so infected that had I waited another six months, I would not have lived to tell the tale. I stayed in a private room and was told not to laugh as that might burst my stitches. Dad and Mum came to see me. Dad always made jokes and this time I really did not want to react to them, but he was so funny that I did have to laugh. It hurt and I told him to stop. Both my parents had been so worried about me and their relief manifested itself in laughter, so I understood why he was joking. I was able to resume my life as soon as my stitches healed, which took a few weeks.

By now my father was an influential rabbi in Anglo-Jewish society. Not only was he the rabbi of the North Western Reform Synagogue in Alyth Gardens, but he was doing many other things as well. Being a great believer in Jewish youth, he was actively involved with and supported two movements: YASGB, the Youth Associations of Great Britain, which is now called Reform Synagogue Youth and RSGB, the Reform Synagogues of Great Britain.

The congregation at Alyth was quite small when he took over, but he built it into a cohesive and exciting community. The congregation increased in numbers as he encouraged the younger members to take an active part in the running of the synagogue and it became vibrant. I was often allowed to take part in the services, as were Jerome and Marcus, my friends and fellow actors in the Lanercost Society. I was also asked to teach the younger pupils Religious Instruction. So I came in each Sunday morning and devised ways of making the lessons interesting for the children. I organised plays for them to perform from the Bible and they seemed to enjoy that immensely.

One summer Sunday, in the early 1950s, I came home from my synagogue class and felt unusually tired. I never normally went to bed during the day, as I had a lot of energy and could not bear the thought of wasting precious time in bed. However, this day I could not keep my eyes open. As I lay in bed, I felt an excruciating pain in my legs. I called my parents and they called Dr Bodian, a member of our congregation who was a paediatrician. He came over immediately and recognised the symptoms of polio. I was taken without delay to the Middlesex Hospital and put in isolation. Everyone who came to see me had to put on a gown and gloves. The actor John Slater came to see me. He was Jewish and knew my father and was the same John Slater who would help me a few years later.

My parents were worried as there was an epidemic of polio going round at that time and 1952 was the worst year by far, affecting mostly children. Three thousand people died from it and many children would not be able to walk again. The problem was that nobody knew what caused polio. There was a theory that it could be passed on in crowds and as I had been to the swimming pool, it was assumed that this was where I had contracted it. Once I realised how serious the situation could be, I was terrified that any chance of me becoming an actress would be ruined if I were to be paralysed in my legs. One could not be an actress sitting in a wheelchair.

After many days in the isolation room, I felt better. I could walk and the fever had gone down. Dr Bodian told my parents that the best thing I had done was to go to bed. Had I tried to walk around when I first experienced the pain in my legs, I might well have been paralysed. When I was getting better in the hospital, I was asked if I could help out in the children's ward. I said I would be glad to. I was so relieved and grateful that I could still walk as normal that I felt I had to give something back. I arrived at the ward and saw a shocking sight. There were children in callipers and others in bed who could not walk at all. Many were crying in pain and my heart went out to them. I spent a lot of time sitting with them and reading to them. It was the least I could do for these poor little ones who seemed to have a bleak future in front of them.

CHAPTER 5
DUAL ATTRACTIONS: MEN AND THE THEATRE

At Alyth, I sometimes went to the celebrations of the Bar or Bat Mitzvah (coming of age) for a boy or girl and also wedding receptions, with my parents. My father had officiated at my Bat Mitzvah at Alyth at the Jewish festival of Shavuot (Pentecost) in 1951, when I was 16. At that time 16 was the age when the ceremony took place. There were usually four or five girls all dressed up for their big day, but this year there was only me and Hannah Isaacs, whose family were friends of ours.

At one Bar Mitzvah celebration, shortly after mine, a young man danced with me and asked me if I would like to come away with him the next weekend and spend time with him on his boat on the Norfolk Broads. I thought he obviously hadn't realised that I was the rabbi's daughter, so I said he should ask my father for his permission. He asked, "Who is your father?" and I pointed out the rabbi. He calmly walked over to him and a few minutes later came back smiling, saying, "That's all right, he said yes." I was flabbergasted and went over to Dad and asked if this were true.

"Why not, you'll have a good time," he said. I was still young and green and had had no experience of men. Dad must have thought it was an innocent invitation, or trusted me to behave. I was still a virgin and although I went out with young men all the time, they were usually Jewish and polite and aware of who my father was, so I didn't get into trouble.

We drove up to the Norfolk Broads in his car. It was the 1950s and not many people had cars never mind a boat, so that was a novelty in itself. We found his boat and it was still daylight, so we boarded and sailed around for a while. We talked and got on fine until he made the comment that when he married, the woman would have to stop work. I was a strong feminist and resented him speaking like that. He also said he would get married in an Orthodox synagogue. He knew my father was a Reform rabbi so this incensed me and I retorted that I would never marry in an Orthodox synagogue. I told him that when I got married, I would want my father to perform my marriage ceremony in his synagogue.

I was hoping at that time to become a good actress and build a career. His chauvinistic remark about not working infuriated me and I took a dislike to his arrogance. Things went from bad to worse when he pretended the boat was stuck on a bank. He did the equivalent to stalling the car. He got us up on the bank and then said we were stuck. I said, "Oh no, we're not!" Angrily, I got up on the bank and heaved, making him push the boat with me and, of course, she slid back into the water.

After that I was ready to go home but I couldn't; we were too far from where we had started and it was getting dark, so we had no alternative but to find a place to sleep that night. We stopped at a hamlet and asked at a little B&B for two rooms. There were no single rooms vacant anywhere. There was only one room to be had in the whole place and that was a room with a double bed. We had to take it, but I did warn him that if he laid one finger on me I would scream until I woke everyone up in the house. We both slept on top of the bed and he never did touch me. We got back to London with my virginity intact. That was the first and last experience with him.

After my dramatic exit from school I was accepted on a year's teaching course at the Central School of Speech and Drama. Dad had insisted on the teaching course to ensure I had some sort of qualification in case I did not succeed as an actress. 'Central' as it is commonly called, is a single faculty drama college and at that time was housed in the Royal Albert Hall. What was great about this was that I was able to continue my friendship with Sir Malcolm Sargent and listen to the rehearsals he conducted in the Hall. At lunchtime, I would sit in and hear Sir Malcolm going through the music with the orchestra for the evening concert. It was fascinating and far more interesting than the concert itself.

I invited Sir Malcolm to my wedding a few years later, but he was ill and couldn't make it. He died of cancer in 1968 but was much too young in spirit and full of energy to die so early. I always remember him with affection. We became firm friends and I used to telephone and see a lot of him at concerts when he and I were in London. He gave me one of his batons to remember him by. As though I could forget him!

After spending a year on the teaching programme, without any acting tuition, I was frustrated and determined to change onto the acting course.

I discussed this with Dad and the principal of Central. They agreed to let me leave, and in 1954 I was accepted for the Preparatory Academy for the Royal Academy of Dramatic Art (PARADA) located in Highgate. At last I was on an acting course and learning all about the techniques of stage and film craft. At the end of the year's course we put on a play. It was *A Midsummer Night's Dream* and I played Puck. It was most enjoyable. Rodney Bewes was on the course with me and later he went on to star in *The Likely Lads* on TV. I did enjoy my time there, but when it came to being accepted for the Royal Academy of Dramatic Art, I was told they deferred you for another year so that they could get more fees for the extra year at PARADA. I wasn't going to fall for that and couldn't afford it anyway, so I left.

In 1955 at the end of the course, I managed to get a job in the West End, playing a maid and understudying the juvenile lead, Constance Wake in *The Pet Shop*. This was supposed to be a follow up to Warren Chatham-Strode's play *The Guinea Pig*, which had been so successful in the West End.

Before transferring to the West End, *The Pet Shop* had a short provincial tour, during which I met the young, good-looking actor in the cast called Peter Myers. He and I got on well and became friendly. This went on for a while, but eventually it got to the time when we wanted to go further. He asked me whether I had ever slept with a man. Remembering the Norfolk Broads, I said innocently that I had slept with a man, thinking that was what he meant. He then began to embrace me and took off my clothes and proceeded to make love to me. As he got to the point, I cried out in pain and he realised I was a virgin. He asked me why I had said I'd slept with a man if I hadn't. I told him about my experience on the Norfolk Broads and he roared with laughter. He was extraordinarily gentle with me and introduced me to the delights of lovemaking over several days. I have never forgotten him as he made it so enjoyable and I am sure one's first experience is crucial. What a lovely man.

We did transfer to the St Martins Theatre in London's West End, but unfortunately, the play did not do anything like as well as *The Guinea Pig*. It lasted all of two weeks. To add insult to injury, while we were having such a hard time, with empty seats in our auditorium, the theatre next door was opening with Agatha Christie's *The Mousetrap* and was packing in the public. It was heartbreaking and because of that I've never wanted to see *The Mousetrap*. To this day, I never have.

While we were playing in London, the actor John Slater came to see our show. By this time we knew it was closing, so he suggested I come and work with him and Brian Rix at the Whitehall Theatre. The play running there at the time was called *Reluctant Heroes*, a farce about the army. There I learned the ropes of producing sound effects that were employed at that time. We used a complicated sound effects machine called a panatrope, on which different records with various sound effects were made. Different records had to be used at certain cues. Thank goodness it was a farce we were doing, as I occasionally got the gunshot effects record mixed up with the wind sound record. However, in spite of this, the show was a great success. We went on to do a provincial tour of the play. The star of the show was Wally Patch, and he was kind to me as a newcomer.

One week we found ourselves in Glasgow and another actress and I had digs together. We came in late one night after our performance at the theatre and found the landlady still up. She had taken a fancy to us and made it clear what she wanted. She chased us round the dining room table and the next day we swiftly found new digs!

It was a lovely cast and we all got on so well with each other. There I met Andrew Sachs, a fellow German Jew and a gentle man. He was a bit diffident then. Now, of course, he is best known for his role as Manuel in the TV series *Fawlty Towers*. He and Anthony Booth played the soldiers. Anthony Booth was on tour with his wife Gail who had their small baby with them. They called her Cherie and I remember cradling her in my arms. Many years later she would become a household name as the wife of Prime Minister, Tony Blair. Clive Brooks was also in the cast, but because there was already an actor with the same name, Clive had to change his. He got a telephone directory and opened it randomly and the name Exton was the name he chose from the page, so Clive Exton he became. He married a lovely girl who was in the cast with us, called Mara. Years later I noticed, when I saw the credits for David Suchet's *Poirot* that Clive wrote most of the scripts.

After the evening performance, a number of us staying in the same digs would sit and have supper and chat. We all opened up and talked about things that affected us. One of our friends in the show said how difficult life was for him because he was a homosexual and, of course, at that time it was not only frowned upon but also illegal. He said he didn't want to be like that and so never had sex at all. How times change, but I have never forgotten the pain he suffered.

At the end of two marvellous years with *Reluctant Heroes* I went on tour with a play called *Bad Girl*. Ivor Burgoyne directed and Simone Silva played the lead. Her claim to fame was that she had discarded her bikini top in front of Robert Mitchum. Later, one of the reviews said that in order for her to make another claim to fame, she'd have to take off her bikini bottoms as well, as she'd never do it with her acting. I played her innocent little sister who becomes pregnant without having had intercourse.

One of the theatres we played was the Glasgow Empire. This was an old theatre and there was a bar at the back of the stalls. Great, just what we needed! People getting drunk and laughing and chatting while we were trying to perform. It was fatal for my scenes with Simone, which had her playing up to the audience and making a farce out of what was supposed to be a serious situation. She played all the scenes for laughs. One night she turned up completely incapable and could not remember her lines. I spent the entire act saying, "I suppose you want to know…." and then answering myself with my own lines. It was seats-of-your-pants stuff all evening, but the audience never realised what was going on. We had hoped the play would come to the West End, but it got such lousy reviews, it never happened.

Before I landed my first role as an actress, I tried to see people who might give me a job. I had just completed my stage training and felt I should meet as many producers as possible. To this end, I was waiting one day in the ante room of number 1 Piccadilly, in London, to see the producer/director Alexander Korda. I was on my own in an impressive high-ceilinged room, when this handsome man approached me and introduced himself as Douglas Fairbanks Jr.

Douglas Fairbanks Jr. was well known in London society. As an actor (following in his famous father's footsteps) he had starred in over 70 movies. But he was also a raconteur, a diplomat (for the USA) and all round man-about-town. He split his time between London and his homes in America. I recommend his autobiography *The Salad Days* which shines a light on an earlier age of movie glamour.

Mr Fairbanks said Mr Korda had asked him to assist me with a view to helping me professionally. He offered me a coffee and we started talking. So began a friendship that lasted for many years. He had his offices near Green Park in Piccadilly and we'd go and see exhibitions together and meet his friends. He didn't get me any work, but his contacts were invaluable and did help me in my career.

At about the time of the Christine Keeler affair, Doug suggested I accompany him to Cliveden, the now infamous country house, for a weekend. Little did I know that the scandal involving John Profumo, Keeler and Mandy Rice-Davies would soon break. As it happens, I didn't go, as by that time I was married and wasn't prepared to enter into any naughtiness with anyone. Doug had said he wanted to introduce me to Sir Laurence Olivier but was afraid he would want to seduce me. I did point out that it takes two to tango, and it never happened.

Later on, when George (who became my second husband) came into my life. I introduced him to Doug and we all met together quite often in London.

Now that I was back in London I went regularly to synagogue services. The congregation had grown extensively and so successful was my father's ministry at Alyth, that in 1957, when the senior rabbi of the West London Synagogue retired, he was asked to succeed him. This was the most important synagogue in the Progressive Movement, in other words the non-Orthodox branch of Judaism. Among his congregation were Jewish families who were household names in the arts and business world, such as the Grade family. I met Sammy Davis Jr. at the High Holy Days services one year. This refers to the two holiest festivals of the Jewish year – Rosh Hashanah (New Year) and ten days later, Yom Kippur (Day of Atonement).

While my father was at the West London Synagogue, one of the families in the congregation was the Winner family. Michael Winner's parents invited my parents and me to their home sometimes and I spent time in the garden with Michael. We got on well. I teased him a lot when he boasted and said that he would be a millionaire by the time he was 30, but I believed him as not only were his parents rich, but he was a go-getting person even then. He was friendly enough but not attractive to me. I seem to remember I was a bit bossy with him.

Many years later, I was asked to revoice an actress in a film he directed called *Hannibal Brooks*. By this time he was a famous film director. I had not seen him since the visits to his parents' garden from our youth and I just reverted to that relationship. We got on fine. When I work on the post-synchronisation of the films on which I am engaged, I am a bit of a perfectionist, so when Michael thought a 'take' was good, I sometimes insisted that I do it again. He was kind to me and let me have my way. I didn't realise that by this time he had a name in the film industry for being a difficult person to work with, but I found him most amenable. When he was out of the room, the sound engineer and others in the studio said they were amazed at the way I interacted with him and how he treated me with respect. I told them that we had met as young people and always got on well and there was nothing strange about it.

However, in his autobiography, Michael writes about an episode that, as far as I can remember, never took place. He says that he took a rabbi's daughter to the pictures and that she more or less seduced him. The reference to Monica (my name before I became Nikki) and revoicing work suggests I am the 'daughter' in question. If that is so, I can honestly say that Michael must have dreamed the whole thing. This is one girl he didn't get! Anyway there it is and Michael has more than fulfilled his ambition of becoming a millionaire. I wish him well.

By now I was seeing many men friends and some were Jewish and some were not. I was very aware that I had to marry a Jew, as my father would not have tolerated my marrying a Gentile. Famous non-last words as we shall see later!

Me, Mum and Dad at a function.

Glamour mode 1

CHAPTER 6
PREGNANCY, ABORTION AND MARRIAGE

All the time I was on tour, one particular male friend, Helmut Jondorf – who was known as Globby in his family– kept turning up at the stage doors of the theatres we were playing in and taking me out when we were in London. This went on for one or two years. He was a German Jew like me and I had met him at the youth group at the West London Synagogue. Shortly after the end of *Bad Girl* he asked me to marry him. I said yes, because he was from my world and I thought we had the best chance of making a go of it. It was also to allow my parents the opportunity to hold their heads high that their actress daughter, who was a rebel and expected to blot her copybook, was actually marrying a Jewish boy. I was fond of him; he looked after me and I felt protected by him, but with hindsight I was much too immature to have committed myself to anyone. However, we became engaged in June 1956.

Sometime after the engagement I discovered to my horror that I was pregnant. This was the 1950s and abortion was illegal. But how could I, the daughter of a rabbi, walk down the aisle of her father's synagogue with a big tummy? No way.

In any case, at that time my father was involved in a battle of his own. Before he fled Berlin, he had witnessed Kristallnacht when, in November 1938, the Nazis smashed all the windows of Jewish shops and businesses, burnt synagogues and books, destroying anything Jewish. He swore that if he survived he would help revive Judaism. Hitler would not have a posthumous victory. Dad vowed that he would build a college for the training of future rabbis and teachers of Judaism.

Now that he had survived and made a name for himself in Anglo-Jewry, he was ready to found his college. But he still had to persuade his prominent rabbinical colleagues to support the forming of a Jewish theological college to train teachers and rabbis. To his frustration and horror there was much opposition to his plan. It was felt there would not be sufficient students to make such a college viable and there was also concern that it would cost more money than could be raised by the Reform Movement. While Dad was still at Alyth in the late 1950s, the senior rabbi of West London Synagogue was Rabbi Harold Reinhart. He was the most influential rabbi in the Reform Movement and he opposed Dad's vision. Reinhart was American and the Hebrew Union College in Cincinnati was where our UK students got their training. Although Reinhart feared there would not be enough students or money to make the project feasible, it was his negative attitude that my father found the most difficult to stomach. Dad had many rows with him and used to come home feeling and looking drained.

I remember talking to one of Dad's colleagues and a good friend, Rabbi Arthur Katz. He told me he used to sit outside Rabbi Reinhart's office and hear the furious arguments between my father and Reinhart. But Dad had sworn to create a college for future generations and he was not going to be put off.

Fortunately, his good friend Sir Leonard Montefiore decided to give the necessary money to start the college. What a welcome relief that was. Dad had finally got his way and his beloved Leo Baeck College was founded in 1956. Rabbi Lionel Blue, one of the college's first students, always says it should have been named the Van Der Zyl College, but Baeck had supported Dad and encouraged him, and so Dad wanted to honour his teacher by calling it by his name. This has confused many people who mistakenly presume it was Leo Baeck who founded it. The college started life in the basement rooms of the West London Synagogue. It went through many stages of accommodation before Leonard Montefiore provided the money to purchase the Manor House in East End Road in North London. Since then it has been enlarged and is now the headquarters of the Reform and Liberal Movements, incorporating the interfaith group, Kindergarten and Bet Limmud (House of Learning). It is now called The Sternberg Centre due to the financial generosity of Sir Sigmund Sternberg, which permitted the growth and establishment of the Progressive Movement. Peter Levy was similarly an incredibly generous donor. The college has been fortunate in having so many generous patrons and friends over the years, too numerous to mention. It is now a thriving institution and at the time of writing, it has ordained over 150 rabbis, as well as providing training for religious educators.

In 1956 when the college opened, Dad was exhausted after fighting the lengthy battles, yet he was to become the first principal. Not only was he recruiting teachers and students for the college and preparing courses of study, he was, at the same time, also the head of the largest Reform congregation in Europe. He had enough on his plate and I didn't want to cause any further upset at that stage by announcing I was pregnant. But I felt that there was no way I could keep the baby.

I called a woman friend who knew about these things and she gave me the name of someone who could help. When I phoned I had to use a password and explain how many 'baskets' I had. This was to tell her how many weeks pregnant I was. She gave me an address in the East End of London along with a date and time for the procedure.

I was anxious about the whole idea. Abortion was illegal and though I was still living at home, neither my mother nor my father had any idea I was pregnant, never mind that I was preparing to have a termination. My fiancé Globby accompanied me to the front door of the East End location at the appointed time, but I went in on my own. My heart was pounding as I had heard such dreadful stories about things going wrong. I was terrified.

I was shown in and saw immediately that the inside of the house was spotless. The room I was ushered into was like an operating theatre, completely sterile and I was made to feel at ease. The lady told me that she was a midwife and explained that she performed abortions to prevent unwanted children coming into the world. She felt she was helping women like me in my circumstances. She told me step by step exactly what would happen after she had carried out the procedure. She said in so many hours such-and-such would happen and not to worry as that was quite normal. It put my mind at ease.

In trepidation I decided to phone my GP and tell him what I'd done. I was not sure how he would respond to my illegal action, but bless him, he was helpful and said I should keep in touch, which I did through all the stages the midwife had outlined. My doctor asked me what had come away from me and I told him that two little foetuses had washed away. At that point, he said I would have been carrying twins and if it would comfort me to know, he personally didn't think I would have carried them to full term as I had lost so much weight in the first month or two after falling pregnant. This was a great relief to me as I felt incredibly guilty at what I had done, even though I could not see any other way out at that time.

Later I heard that another woman, who had the same lady perform her abortion, had panicked and reported her. My well-meaning midwife was severely punished with a jail sentence. I was terribly upset as she had been meticulous with her cleanliness and hygiene. She only acted out of compassion for young women in a precarious situation. Thank goodness this sort of thing doesn't happen any more.

In contrast to the traumatic abortion, some time later in November 1956, I was asked to audition for the first English performance of *The Saint of Bleecker Street*, an opera in three acts by Gian Carlo Menotti for BBC Television. I was summoned to appear before Rudolph Cartier, an Austrian television director, and Ernest Maxim, a BBC Light Entertainment producer, to audition for a small part. Cartier had been a screenwriter and a film director in Berlin and was once described as 'a true pioneer of television'. I was thrilled when I was told my audition was successful as this would be the first time I would be on television, even though it was just a walk-on part. The production was broadcast live from the BBC TV studios. In those days there was no such thing as pre-recordings. It was nail-biting for everyone, both actors and technicians, because if anything went wrong, we had to continue regardless.

I had met Ernest Maxim with my mother years before. Mum used to accompany my singing at home when I sang German nursery rhymes and songs. We thought it might be suitable for a slot in a light entertainment TV programme. Ernest loved the idea, but said it was too soon after the war and people were not ready for anything German. Had he suggested we sing English songs for children, it might have turned out differently but, as it was, nothing came of it. The story of my life, one might say.

Getting back to my forthcoming marriage, my father's great friend and mentor, Rabbi Leo Baeck was supposed to perform the ceremony for us, with Dad, but he died in the months before it was to take place.

He had been my father's teacher and mentor in Berlin and they had been through so much together. My father didn't make friends easily, but Baeck was a close friend. Dad was devastated at his death and I could only imagine what he was going through. It affected me as well and I felt for Dad. This was the funeral of someone special and dear to my father. He didn't call his theological college The Leo Baeck College for nothing!

My fiancé and his family all came to the funeral. On the way back from the service, I was in the car with Globby, his father Willy and stepmother Betty. Willy started telling jokes and laughing. I was still in an emotional state of mind rather like when you have just seen a moving film on TV and you are still in the midst of those feelings, when the announcer comes on and in a raucous voice advertises what's on next. I was shocked and said something like "Willy, don't make fun of the dead, you may well be the next person to die." I thought no more of it.

Days before the wedding, my father had asked me if I wanted to change my mind about marrying Globby and I said no. I wondered why he had asked me that, but again thought no more about it.

Globby and I got married on 27th January, 1957. Dad took me down the aisle, said quietly to me "Prepare to meet Thy Hell" (a mischievous play on the name Helmut), and then turned round and performed the marriage ceremony. I looked slim and bride-like going down the aisle and nobody except me and my fiancé knew what had recently taken place. Mum and Dad never did find out.

After our marriage Globby and I went to Switzerland for the honeymoon. We learnt to ski and had a glorious fortnight. We took photos of ourselves and got them printed. When we went back to pick them up, we were told that they had come out well and the assistant said "your daughter looks lovely". Oops, this was not flattering to my husband, but I did look young for my age. A few weeks later, when Globby was at work and I was in the flat on my own, a man came round to read the gas meter. On seeing me he asked if my mother was at home. I was indignant and informed him I was the mistress of the house. He smiled and apologised.

After a lovely honeymoon, we came back to the ghastly news that my new husband's father had suddenly died. I suppose it must have been a heart attack, but there had not appeared to be anything wrong with him. My words had come true and I felt somewhat guilty for what I had said to him in the car at Leo Baeck's funeral.

One night soon after his father's death, Globby opened up to me and cried. I thought that was a good sign and tried to comfort him and held him in my arms. The next morning he stiffly apologised for crying and said that it would never happen again. I was amazed, hurt and confused that he was ashamed of having shown emotion or affection. I realised then that Globby hated any sign of emotion. I think to him it was a sign of weakness. How sad.

During the first year of our marriage, Globby's stepmother Betty felt she needed him to be with her almost every evening, so after work he would come home, have his supper that I prepared for us and then take off to see her. Not only was I alone during the day, trying to get used to my new situation, I was also on my own every evening as well. I had never been entirely on my own for long periods before and was not used to it. I no longer felt protected by Globby, but lonely and abandoned. I craved warmth and love.

The physical side of our marriage also completely lacked any feelings of love or tenderness. I became increasingly unhappy, and everything seemed to pile up on top of me. After having endured a year of extreme loneliness and a frustrating sex life, I got up the courage to leave him. Just as I finally decided to do so, I realised I was pregnant again. This time I was going to have my baby and give it all the love in the world.

In the 1950s you didn't leave your husband if you were pregnant and had no means of supporting yourself, so I decided to make the best of things and try to make the marriage work.

During the summer of 1958, while I was pregnant, Mum and Dad took me on a driving holiday through France and Spain. We went to a little fishing village on the Mediterranean coast called Cadaques, where the artist Salvador Dali lived. We met a pleasant family with whom we got friendly. The daughter was the same age as me and we got on well. She knew Dali and one day she introduced me to him and I and my parents were invited to his home and studio. When Dali opened the front door, we were met in the hall by a life-size stuffed bear on his hind legs. It was quite a moment. His lounge overlooked the sea and his book shelves were so high up that a ladder was needed to get to them. On the way upstairs on the left-hand side wall, Dali had photos of all the dictators – Franco, Hitler, Mussolini etc. He also patted my backside as we were moving upstairs. I was not amused! When we got to the top, he showed us his latest painting of the Madonna and child. I asked him why he had a picture on the easel of a Madonna and child and he pretended not to speak English, although I knew he was fluent. It was a bizarre experience and one that I've never forgotten.

During that trip with my parents we toured around in Dad's car. From Cadaques, we drove on to Barcelona. We booked into a hotel and while we were there, I had a phone call asking me to come back to London to work. How the producers found me remains a mystery. They asked me to do some more revoicing on the film *Tale of Two Cities* in which I had revoiced Marie Versini playing the part of Marie Gabelle, before going on holiday with my parents. That was my first big revoicing job. Dirk Bogarde played the lead and Marie Versini was the girl with whom he shares his prison cell and who accompanies him in the cart which carries them to the gallows. It was a remake of the film first shot in 1935, with Ronald Coleman. Now they needed me back. They arranged a flight and paid for my ticket. I was loath to leave my parents but had little choice. The flight back to Heathrow was a nightmare. I was sick all the way home and felt dreadful. I went to Pinewood three days running and revoiced the bits that were necessary. I was almost due to give birth and quite uncomfortable, but the show must go on, even in post-production!

My own biological show started a few days later.

At five o'clock during the night of Sunday, 16th November 1958, I woke up, went to the toilet and realised that I was in labour. My contractions were coming every five minutes. Globby rang the maternity home in Hampstead, where I was to give birth and ordered a taxi. We lived in Temple Fortune then, not far from Hampstead, and it was not long before I was ensconced in the delivery room. As the contractions were so close together the birth should have taken place quite soon after my arrival. However, I was struggling to get my baby born and it took the rest of that night and the whole of the next day for her to make her debut. It was taking so long because she was emerging face up instead of down and I was very small, so she had a problem. I was exhausted, but my beautiful little girl Kerry Lyn was finally delivered to us at 8.30 pm on 17th November.

Although I had my differences with my husband, he had been in the delivery room with me for all those hours, even though I hadn't realised it at the time. This was good of him and I was grateful. He told the family that she was the sweetest baby. Because of her struggle to come out of me, her head was elongated, but she still looked gorgeous. The elongation only lasted a few days and then her head recovered to the right size. I wasn't allowed to breastfeed her for the first day because she was shocked and bruised, poor little thing, but I was thrilled with her. In those days we were not sent home as early as today's mothers. I stayed at the maternity home for 11 days after her birth, but in my case it was a bit longer than usual as the midwife wanted to make sure Kerry was well enough to come home with me.

Globby had a brother called Werner whom I first met when our families had got together at the engagement party. He was quite different to my fiancé. He was a bohemian type of person, and drove everywhere on his powerful motorbike, clad in black leathers. He was a cancer research scientist, specialising in different aspects of the disease.

He had an amusing turn of phrase and I took to him immediately. Globby and I saw a lot of him as he used to come round regularly to our flat in Temple Fortune. He became a good friend to me. When my son Darrell was born, Werner gave me an original painting by Mary Talbot. The subject was the face of Michelangelo's David and it was done in such a way that one had to spend time studying the painting before realising that it actually was a face. It has butterflies around it and is quite beautiful. I continued my friendship with Werner after my divorce from Globby, when I introduced him to George. Ironically and tragically, Werner died of cancer at much too young an age. I still miss him to this day. He left a scholarly wife and three girls, two of whom were twins. Before he died he asked me to stay in touch with them, but somehow we drifted apart.

Me and Dad with newborn Kerry, 1958

Rabbi Dad

CHAPTER 7
MY BOND YEARS

After Kerry's birth I spent some time at home with her before going back to work, which was never full time anyway. I had, by now, acquired an agent, the Harry Harbour and Jill Coffey Agency. They had got me a few acting jobs here and there, including the one I had just completed before Kerry's birth.

I also managed to get a small part in the film *Conspiracy of Hearts* (1960) as a nun. The part played by Sylvia Syms as a novice nun, calls on her to sing a Hebrew prayer. As someone who sang in Hebrew in my synagogue choir every Saturday, it is ironic that my language skills were not called on and I was mute throughout the film. It is even more ironic that throughout my subsequent acting career I would be known, within the film industry, only for my voice. But that's show business for you!

I suppose one way to get on in pictures as an actress is to sleep with the person who is most likely to give you a part in a film. The casting couch is an inevitable part of the system. However, I was determined that I would get on in the film business without the dreaded couch syndrome. I felt that if my acting wasn't good enough to get me a part, why should my sexual exploits be any better? Quite apart from the fact that I had been brought up as a proper Jewish woman who didn't cheat on her husband, I thought in a practical way too. Suppose the person who wanted to bed me in return for a lead in a film wasn't impressed with me afterwards for whatever reason and I still didn't get the part, I would not only be cheap but totally humiliated as well. I still had to live with myself!

Michael Relph was the director of *Conspiracy of Hearts* and it was at the end of one day's filming at Pinewood that he offered me a lift to Uxbridge station. After I got into his car he pounced on me. I was surprised and horrified, so I thought quickly and told him that I always fell madly in love with anyone who kissed me, or had sex with me. I told him I would follow them, telephone them at home and generally make a nuisance of myself. I said I couldn't help it – it was a kind of addiction! He believed me and suddenly he had to be somewhere else and was sorry that he couldn't give me a lift to Uxbridge after all. What a relief! My acting ability had helped me out of that one.

I referred earlier to my language skills. The way I got into revoicing was through meeting the actor Robert Rietti when I was 16. My father asked him to take part in a poetry evening at his synagogue, Alyth, in which I was also reading. I was nervous to be appearing with him as he was an established actor and I was in awe of him. A little while later he asked my dad if he could take me out, which he did. It was all quite proper and he introduced me to his charming father, Victor. Robert and his father were well-known Italian/ Jewish actors. We used to call Victor 'Papa' and he and Robert were both kind to me. Robert and I worked together for many years after Papa's death. We are still in touch even now.

Victor and Robert specialised in dubbing foreign films into English. They took me under their wing and I learned much from them. I started to work with them in the Rudolph Steiner Theatre in Baker Street. They taught me the art of dubbing, which is the correct term for the recording and replacing of the actor's words in foreign films. Dubbing in English films refers to adding sound effects, such as squeaky doors, creaky stairs, footsteps, etc. This is different to replacing the voice of actors speaking the dialogue in English. The proper term for this is post-synchronisation, or revoicing as it is usually called.

In dubbing, the English translation of the foreign words of the lines that have to be spoken were written underneath the moving picture. When the words were close together it meant the pace was fast and when the words were written further apart, it meant they should be read slowly. There was a vertical bar going from one side of the screen to the other and one started speaking the lines when the bar appeared and finished the sentence when the bar reached the other side. It also had to be acted properly and the English words had to match as closely as possible the foreign words, quite apart from the movement of the actor's lips. It is an art form and not as easy as it might sound.

De Lane Lea is a well-known post-production company that specialises in dubbing and revoicing artistes. Louis Elman was the director in charge of voice production. Robert had worked there for some years and introduced me to him. I then worked with Louis and Robert and many other actors, such as Peter Bowles, Pauline Collins, Annie Ross, the famous jazz singer, Rick Jones and others whose names I have forgotten. We worked on numerous foreign films, TV series, children's films and documentaries.

As De Lane Lea is so widely respected in the film industry, producers approach the company to find actors to revoice actors in their films whose voices are unsuitable for one reason or another.

In the early 1960s, my agent sent me for an oral audition at Pinewood Studios. What I didn't know then was that the producers of a film, then in production, had first contacted Louis Elman at De Lane Lea to find someone to revoice the leading actress. Louis recommended me and told them I was the best person to do the job. The usual fee for a revoicing session at that time was £15, but Louis got them to increase it to £25. This doesn't sound much today, but then it was unheard of to get that for a single session. So I have Louis to thank for that.

The film that had just finished shooting was introducing an unknown foreign actress called Ursula Andress and a little known British actor called Sean Connery. The film was *Dr. No*, based on the 1958 spy novel of the same name by Ian Fleming. As John Cork relates in his book *James Bond The Legacy*, co-authored with Bruce Scivally, Ursula had been hired because Cubby Broccoli, one of the producers, had been impressed by photos he had seen of her playing in the surf wearing a T-shirt. He was warned by casting director Max Arnow that 'she had a voice like a Dutch comic' but that didn't deter Cubby. So now the producers wanted someone to revoice Ursula as they realised her voice was not appropriate for the sexy part she was playing. I knew nothing of this background when I went to Pinewood and did the test.

Sometime afterwards I was told I had got the job and so I went to the Head Office of EON Productions in the West End to meet the director, Terence Young. I was an actress and always wanted to appear in films. I asked if there might be a role for me in the next film. He said "No, I'm afraid you wouldn't stop the traffic, Nikki."

I was slim and was not conventionally curvy up top if you know what I mean, so the blondes with big busts were getting the juicy roles. It had nothing to do with acting, hence the need for revoicing! However, the good-looking young man in the corner came up to me and said in a loud voice, "I'd stop the traffic for you any day." That voice belonged to Sean Connery, who was to be the first James Bond in the series. I appreciated his support for me in front of Terence Young.

Having succeeded in getting the voice audition for Ursula, as soon as the filming was finished, I was called to the sound studio at Pinewood Studios, to revoice her.

So how do you go about revoicing the whole part of the actress in an English-speaking film?

The actress's part is cut up into what are called 'loops' and each loop is separately performed. Hence, the process is also known in the business as 'looping'.

The problem with Ursula Andress was that not only did she have a strong Swiss-German accent, but she tended to put the emphasis of a word on the wrong syllable, making it difficult to match the lip movement. Her voice was also deeper than mine, so I had to drop my voice as well.

Inevitably, the producers would want to distribute the film in the USA. They felt her accent might be too difficult for the American audience to understand and in any case, it wasn't sexy enough. I was asked to give her a 'mid-Atlantic' accent. I didn't quite know what they were after, but thought they wanted a foreign sound with maybe a pinch of Americanism whipped in. Getting it right was crucial. That first time was the most difficult for me and I kept trying different ways to perfect it. That took ages, but finally they and I were satisfied that the voice was what they wanted.

One of the difficulties is that you have to hear the original voice speaking the lines through headphones in order to remember the words of the scene. (That's why a script is not used when post-synching.) It is also important not to copy the same inflection of the words as the actress, as that is precisely what the producers and director want changed. I had to perform the scenes as though I was on the set myself. When all the loops of the film have been revoiced, they are stitched back together again and the result is that the actress is speaking with my voice. This was when I met and worked with Norman Wanstall, the sound editor on *Dr. No* and subsequent Bond films.

The first time you hear my voice in *Dr. No* is when the radio operator in the Kingston, Jamaica office of the British Intelligence Station Chief, John Strangways, is trying to contact London. She hears a noise and turns and shrieks when she sees the three armed intruders and is then shot dead. That voice-over sequence lasts all of 28 seconds and is the first female voice heard in the EON production Bond films.

The next time you hear me is when the character Sylvia Trench, played by Eunice Gayson, is at the gambling table at the Le Cercle Club in London.

It's the first time you hear a female voice addressing 007 in the Bond films. You hear me say the famous line: "I admire your luck, Mr...?"

He, equally famously, responds, "Bond ... James Bond". This scene is also our introduction to 007 James Bond as played by the panther-like Sean Connery.

The conversation between me, as Honey Ryder, and Bond happens in the memorable scene when she emerges from the sea wearing the iconic white bikini with a knife strapped to her thigh, singing 'Underneath the Mango Tree' with my voice. This was already quite a long way into the film. The actual words spoken in the released film are:

Bond: (*Sings the same tune.*)
Honey: Who's that?
Bond: It's all right .... I'm not supposed to be here either, I take it you're not. Are you alone?
Honey: What are you doing here? Looking for shells?
Bond: No, I'm just looking.
Honey: Stay where you are.
Bond: I promise I won't steal your shells.
Honey: I promise you, you won't either. Stay where you are.
Bond: I can assure you my intentions are strictly honourable.

And so one of cinemas most unforgettable scenes unfolds. It would become etched in audience memories around the world and James Bond would become an established favourite hero and go on to make a fortune for the producers.

In a 2010 *Radio Times* poll, Ursula Andress was voted the top film siren according to men. Well, in Greek mythology the Sirens were dangerous, seductive creatures who lured nearby sailors to shipwreck with their enchanting music and voices. So whose was the seductive siren voice that so enraptured the voters? Thanks guys!

The soundtrack quoted above differs slightly from the draft screenplay dated 8th January 1962. This is not surprising because, as so often happens, changes are made during shooting. The screenplay describes Honey as 'naked except for a wisp of home-made bikini and a broad leather belt with an undersea knife in a sheath'. (Note, the screenplay spells her name as Ryder, not Rider as it often appears.) Here is the dialogue from the screenplay, with voice directions:

Bond: (appreciating what is seen. In a moment he takes up the calypso refrain)

Honey: (terrified whisper) Who's that?

Bond: (disarmingly) It's all right ... I'm not supposed to be here either. Are you alone?

Honey: (suspiciously) What are you doing here? Looking for shells?

Bond: No – just looking.

Honey: You stay where you are.

(Her eyes still on his, she stoops and gathers up the pile she has collected.

Bond: (laughs) I promise you I won't steal any of them.

Honey: (darkly) I promise you, you won't either.

Bond (advances further)

Honey: (sharply ... hand flying to knife) Stay where you are...

Bond: (easily) Now, put that away. My intentions are strictly honourable.

(He comes up to her. She still holds the knife at the ready.)

Bond: What's your name?

Honey: (after a pause) Ryder.

It is often thought that the first screen 'Bond Girl' was either Ursula or Eunice Gayson, but that is wrong. That honour goes to the actress Linda Christian who died in 2011. She starred in the 1954 CBS television adaptation of Ian Fleming's debut novel *Casino Royale* in which Barry Nelson appeared as Secret Agent 'Jimmy Bond', with Peter Lorre as the villain Le Chiffre. Linda was born in Mexico, the daughter of a Dutch oil executive and his German-Mexican wife. I wonder if she needed revoicing!

At this stage the producers of *Dr. No* had no idea whether their film of Ian Fleming's book would be successful, but they must have liked what I was doing because I was then asked to revoice nearly every other female in the film, which included Eunice Gayson. I didn't revoice Miss Moneypenny and one Chinese girl. The revoicing only happens after shooting the film is concluded, during post-production. By that time the budget has usually been used up, so there is never much money left.

As I stated earlier, I received £25 for one session. Once the voice was right, I usually only took one or two sessions to revoice an entire film. Perhaps that is why I was used so much. I was good value and known in Pinewood as 'one-take Nikki'.

Of course the producers weren't to realise how popular and financially successful their first film was going to be, but as soon as they did, they decided to carry on making all the Ian Fleming books into feature films.

Ursula's subsequent sexy reputation was partly based on my voice and this would have some unforeseen consequences. In 1963, she went to America to make the film *Four for Texas* and as Roger Moore told me later, nobody had told the producers that I had revoiced Ursula in *Dr. No*. When they and the starring actors, Frank Sinatra and Dean Martin, went to pick her up from the airport, she walked sexily down the steps from the plane, but when she opened her mouth to speak, they nearly fell off their horses. They were expecting the soft, seductive voice I had given her. Instead, they heard her natural thick Swiss accent and they were horrified. The producers of the Bond film, Harry Salzman and Cubby Broccoli, were nearly taken to court on account of that incident.

In the same year, filming began on the next Bond film *From Russia With Love*. One day I had a phone call from Peter Hunt, the film editor, who said he was sending a limousine for me in order to do a film test for the main part in the movie. The limo never turned up and I heard no more. I found out later that the producers, Harry Salzman and Cubby Broccoli, had decided they didn't like Daniela Bianchi in the part and wanted me for the lead. However, she had already signed the contract and it would have cost them too much to get out of it. At least they didn't ask me to revoice Daniela! (That was done by Barbara Jefford, also uncredited.) Instead, I again revoiced Eunice Gayson who plays the part of Sylvia Trench, Bond's occasional girlfriend.

In that year, the same company – EON Productions – filmed *Call Me Bwana* at Elstree, with Bob Hope and Anita Ekberg. At the end of the shooting, when Bob Hope was back in the States, the film was sent over to Cubby and Harry for post-production. They wanted me to insert my voice in some of Anita's individual sentences, which they felt were not quite right. Bob Hope was not to know that this was happening, so I had to match her voice perfectly. It was one of the most difficult jobs I ever did, as they mixed my revoiced words with her original words. After the massive effort it took to match Anita's voice, the tape was sent back to Bob. One of the best compliments I ever received came when Hope cabled back to the producers saying, "See, I told you Anita didn't need revoicing!" My contribution had, yet again, gone undetected.

In 1964 EON Productions were looking for a suitable actor to play the role of the villain Goldfinger in the film of the same name. This was the third in the James Bond series and it would be a blockbuster with a budget equalling the two previous films combined. Gert Fröbe was then an established German actor, but so far had not appeared in any British or American films. The producers had been impressed by his portrayal of a serial child killer in a Swiss-German film called *Es geschah am hellichten Tag* (*It Happened in Broad Daylight*) and signed him up to play the gold tycoon Auric Goldfinger. I first met Gert and his wife Beate at Pinewood and then, a couple of days later, met them again at the Westbury Hotel where they were staying. Because I was bilingual I was asked by the director Guy Hamilton to look after them and help them find a flat.

Gert was in his 60s at the time and I was anxious to know what he had been doing in Germany during the war years. After all, my parents and I had to leave Berlin because of the Nazis and some of my family were murdered. When I met him and his wife that was the first question I asked him. He told me that his parents had secretly sheltered some Jews in their house from the Nazis, at the risk of their own lives. I was reassured and decided I would help him with his English. I was engaged as his dialogue coach and I also told him that people might have a problem pronouncing his name and suggested that he drop the umlaut and call himself plain Frobe, which he did. I worked closely with him on the sets and we became firm friends.

One of the outdoor scenes in *Goldfinger* was set at Stoke Poges Golf Club. Sean (Connery) was an expert golfer and between scenes he taught me how to play golf. He always stood up for me if I had any problems with anyone. Indeed, an issue arose when the cast went on location and I felt my job was to be with Gert during the filming of the card-playing scenes in Miami. They told me I couldn't go. Sean fought on my side, but it was no use as the production manager was adamant. I thought it mean that they wouldn't pay for me to accompany the actor and help him with his dialogue just because he was away from Pinewood Studios. I'm quite sure the budget would have stood the strain!

I went through each day's shooting schedule with Gert to prepare his dialogue. In the scene where Bond is tied to the table with a laser about to cut him in two, Bond says: "Do you expect me to talk?"

Goldfinger replies: "No Mr Bond. I expect you to die." Gert delivered the line fairly dramatically at first, but I told him that it would be more effective if he said it in a throwaway manner, which he does in the film. This was how I worked with him. He was an exceptionally fast learner and I was sorry to learn later that he had been revoiced by Michael Collins after filming had been completed. I felt it was a little unfair that this had to be done as it was not at all his fault. The reason I say this is because at the beginning of shooting, his English was not good and unfortunately the scenes he was asked to do then were much longer than at the end of filming, when his English had vastly improved. Had he done the short scenes early on and the longer ones at the end, I am sure he would not have had to be revoiced. However, having said that, Louis Elman suggested Michael Collins, whose voice is uncannily close to Gert's own. If I didn't know better, I would never have realised it wasn't Gert's voice.

The mute villain Oddjob, played by Harold Sakata, was as strong in real life as he appeared in the film. He demonstrated this to us one day by smashing through a pile of bricks with a single stroke of his bare hand. But he was also gentle and a sweet-natured man.

In the finished film, as impressive as the sets look onscreen, it cannot convey the full impact of actually walking on to one of the sets designed by Ken Adam. Stepping into Fort Knox at Pinewood I was blown away by the sheer scale of it. The sound effects in the film were similarly impressive and Norman Wanstall deservedly won the Motion Picture Academy Award Oscar for his skilful work. *Goldfinger* went on to break box office records.

My vocal contribution to *Goldfinger* was revoicing the part of Jill Masterson, the blonde assistant/escort, played by Shirley Eaton. The character famously meets her death through 'skin suffocation' (an utterly fictional medical condition by the way) having been being painted entirely with gold. Incidentally, a different girl was used for the gold-painted body seen in the opening titles and film advertisements.

Gert was a funny man and a brilliant storyteller. He often pretended he was a brass band and without a single instrument, used his voice to be a trumpet and other brass band instruments. Sometimes he, Sean and I had lunch in Pinewood Studios restaurant. It was a gloriously spacious room that would not have looked out of place in a palace, with a high ceiling and wood carvings round the top. I met so many stars there, such as Robert Wagner and Peter Finch. One day I was going up the steps to the restaurant and Peter Finch was coming down. I did a double take when I saw him and promptly tripped on the next step. He helped me up and we exchanged a few words.

On one occasion I even had a go as a stunt woman. This happened when *Carry On Cleo* was being filmed at Pinewood at the same time as *Goldfinger*. I got chatting to Bob Simmons, the stunt man who was doing so much work on the Bond films. He arranged for me to be the stand-in for Amanda Barrie when her scenes were being prepared. My diary for 1964 tells me that on 28th July I had lunch with Gert and his friend Karl Michael Vogler in the Pinewood restaurant and afterwards had a costume fitting for Cleo in readiness for the next day's shooting. This was the legendary scene where Cleo is delivered to Caesar wrapped in a rug. When the rug is opened, Cleo rolls across the floor and crashes into a table which then collapses on her. That happened to me – and my head really did hurt! In the released movie that scene is played at fast speed, so I cannot be sure, but it's probably me. I think Amanda was reluctant to reshoot it after hearing about my injury.

Thunderball, made in 1965, was the fourth James Bond film. The villain Emilio Largo was played by Italian actor Adolfo Celi, but revoiced by my old friend Robert Rietti, also of Italian extraction. Odd world! The producers considered a number of actresses for the part of Dominique 'Domino' Derval, Largo's kept mistress. The list included Julie Christie, Raquel Welch, Faye Dunaway and several relatively unknown European actresses, one of whom was Claudine Auger, a former Miss France. She ended up being the final choice to play the part of Domino. Yet whatever qualities she possessed to win her the role, they didn't include the right voice and so once again I was called on to do my thing in the sound studio. I also revoiced some minor female parts in the film.

Some of the dialogue from the Bond films has entered into my private life with George. One phrase we use from *Thunderball* is 'Vargas behind you' from the scene when Bond is sitting with Domino on the beach and being stalked by her bodyguard. No reason; it's silly, but it amuses us!

In 1966 Hammer Films made *One Million Years B.C.* The film turned out to be one of the company's most expensive and profitable productions. One reason for its success was the casting of Raquel Welch in the part of Loana. The most remembered thing about the film is the publicity shot of her wearing the bikini-styled fur costume. It became a poster classic and propelled Raquel to international sex symbol status.

There was a minimum of scripted dialogue for the film's invented language and Raquel had only three lines of 'speech' in the whole film. Even so, it was felt she couldn't convincingly handle the delivery of phrases like 'Neh, Neh' and 'Akita! Akita!', so I was called to Elstree Studios to do it the proper way, including the many shrieks and groans. *The Guinness Book of Movie Facts & Feats* (1988) says: 'Miss Welch's middle-western accent sounded insufficiently prehistoric and Miss van der Zyl was called in to grunt the straight Neanderthal way'. I liked that!

Interestingly, Ursula Andress had first been offered the role of Leona after starring in the 1965 Hammer film *She* – in which I also replaced her voice.

However, she turned the part down and it was taken by the then unknown Raquel Welch. Either way, you would still hear my voice!

In 1966 Twentieth Century Fox made *The Blue Max* with Ursula Andress playing Countess Kaeti von Klugermann. Even though Ursula was now playing a character which suited her native accent, I was still asked to revoice her. Was this because the film-makers preferred her with the seductive voice I gave her?

The influential Internet Movie Database (IMDb) says of Ursula Andress that she 'spent most of her time faking being an actress'. That may be a bit harsh, but it is true that it was the combination of the alluring screen voice that I gave her complementing her stunning beauty and voluptuous figure which helped win her legions of male fans. As a result, she became the stuff of legends.

In 1967, the fifth Bond film *You Only Live Twice* was made. Apart from the sets constructed at Pinewood, it was filmed almost entirely on location in Japan. The casting of the two main Japanese female parts was difficult because of their limited English. In the end I was called in to revoice Mie Hama who played the pearl-diving girl Kissy Suzuki.

Interestingly, one of the hardest revoicing jobs I ever did had also been for another Japanese actress, Yoko Tani, in the film *Savage Innocents* made in 1960. There was a mixture of French, American and Japanese in Tani's voice and it took me a long time to master her accent. In the end it was fine, but the film was not a success, even though it had a major star, Anthony Quinn. Peter O'Toole, who was at that time relatively unknown, played a Canadian trooper. When O'Toole was revoiced, he objected and had his name removed from the credits, causing a rumpus. So you see, being revoiced can happen even to the best known actors.

I did less work on the subsequent Bond films and was used mostly for smaller parts which needed to be corrected or improved. Maybe they were using more competent actresses by then. In *On Her Majesty's Secret Service* (1969) I revoiced Olympe played by Virginia North. For *Live and Let Die* (1973), the eighth film in the series and the first with Roger Moore as 007, I was asked to revoice some of Jane Seymour's lines as Solitaire. Revoicing part of a performance, rather than the whole, is more testing – as I have already mentioned with respect to Anita Ekberg. This is because, unless the match is absolutely perfect, there is a risk of the replacement voice being detected. But, fortunately, in my case, nobody did.

In *The Man with the Golden Gun* (1974) I revoiced several minor parts but the most memorable was Françoise Therry who played Chew Mee. She was the naked swimming beauty who Bond meets when he is pretending to be the villain Scaramanga (played by Christopher Lee). When she invites Bond to swim with her, he says: "Well, there is only one small problem. I have no swimming trunks." Chew Mee replies: "Neither have I."

Going back to 1960 for a moment, I recall Douglas Fairbanks took me to Shepperton Studios where they were shooting a film called *Guns of Navarone*. Doug's friend David Niven was in it and Doug introduced me to him. He was a real gentleman and we talked a great deal. When we went back to the film set, Anthony Quinn was coming out of a tunnel and when that scene finished, I had the chance to talk to him. I referred to my revoicing Yoko Tani in *Savage Innocents*, but he was not forthcoming. It was not easy talking to him. Perhaps he was unhappy about *Savage Innocents* poor reception and associated me with the film.

I also met Stanley Baker who was charming and while we were talking, Gregory Peck came running out of the tunnel. When that scene finished, he stopped and chatted to me. It was obvious that he found me as attractive as I did him and after we had exchanged a few words together, he invited me to come and have lunch with him at Pinewood in a few weeks' time, when he would start working on his next film. I was absolutely thrilled that Gregory Peck wanted to see me again.

I waited impatiently for the next time I would see him and eventually the day arrived. I took the train to Uxbridge which seemed to take an interminable time and then the bus to the studios. I finally got to the set and knocked on the door. A young man came out and I said I had an appointment with Mr Peck. He asked me to wait and after a few minutes Gregory came to the door and greeted me. He looked as pleased as Punch to see me and he said we'd have lunch in a little while. However, as we were speaking together, Sophia Loren who was co-starring with him in the film, came to the door wanting to know what was going on. When Gregory told her we were going to have lunch together, she pouted and said, "But Gregory, you said you would take me for lunch." I waited to see what he would say. I hoped he would insist that he had made the arrangement with me weeks ago and couldn't let me down, but all he said was that he was terribly sorry, but he would have to go along with Sophia. To say I was upset was an understatement. I was furious and all I could do was to go back home feeling humiliated and miserable. I hated Sophia for being so selfish; after all she was seeing him every day of filming, but I also blamed Gregory for not standing up to her and honouring our long-standing engagement. The film they were shooting was *Arabesque*. Consequently, I have never wanted to see it and have never watched any films in which she starred since then.

Although I have never felt that making loads of money is the be all and end all of life, I was upset at the way I was treated. I got on well personally with Harry Salzman and Cubby Broccoli, the producers of the Bond films. We never had a cross word in all the years that I worked for them. They made a lot of money, helped in part by using my voice, yet I never received any acknowledgment for my work on the Bond films, be it credits or any other sort of recognition, aside from the small fee I earned for the nine films I revoiced. I was never once invited to a premier of a Bond film and even at the time of writing, the successors to the original producers try to pretend I don't exist. By the time of the 20th anniversary of the first Bond film, I was no longer involved in the film industry. As a great deal of fuss was being made about Bond, I decided to let the cat out of the bag and revealed my part in the Bond films to the *Daily Express* journalist, Garth Pearce. They printed a double-page spread about me in March 1983 and the story was syndicated all round the world.

John Cork, the American author and documentary maker, came over to London in 2002 while researching for his book *Bond Girls Are Forever*. He interviewed me because he knew about my significant vocal contributions to the Bond films and wanted to include me. The book blurb promises that it will "… reveal for the first time the true stories …" about the Bond girls. But my name appears nowhere in the book and there is no mention of the fact that many of the pictured Bond girls were revoiced by me. He later told me that he had been constrained from writing about me in the book but did not reveal any names. The only reference to speech is in the description of the famous beach scene when Honey Ryder first confronts Bond. The text refers to the 'grimly confident note in her voice'. In a work of reference I think it does a disservice to film aficionados to deny them the truth.

It could have been that the producers were keen to maintain the illusion of stardom. It might never occur to the audience that the voices they heard did not belong to the faces on the screen. It had to remain a clandestine process.

My film work continued for many years and this is woven into my multi-stranded narrative.

The Bond movies have always been peppered with witty lines and double entendres, and I know there are quite a few 007 jokes in circulation. George came up with this funny twist on the famous Goldfinger laser scene. The premise is this: 008 is a Welsh agent, called Dai (pronounced 'die'). He is captured by Goldfinger's thugs and they drag him to his lair where they glue him to the table top. When struggling, 008 sees Goldfinger approach he says 'Do you expect me to talk Goldfinger?' To which Goldfinger replies: 'No, I expect you to bond, Mr Dai'.

Glamour mode 2

Glamour mode 3

Sultry pose

Sean Connery fooling around on the Goldfinger set.

Gert and me relaxing on the Goldfinger set

CHAPTER 8
MARRIAGE BREAKDOWN

I gave birth to my little boy, Darrell, in 1961. Unlike his sister he came out the right way up and it only took two hours for him to appear. He weighed seven pounds and a few ounces. He was as adorable as his sister. I loved and still love them both dearly, although Darrell has caused quite a lot of grief later in my life, but more on that in another chapter.

Because of my professional work I was not able to be with the children all the time. My husband was also working and so we needed to have someone to take care of them on days when I was not home. We decided to engage an au pair. This was different from when I was exchanging visits with my French au pair in our respective homes. Now an au pair was expected to help take care of the children and look after the house in exchange for board and lodging and a modest wage.

When the children were a little older, I was invited by Douglas Fairbanks Jr. and Joel Spector to spend a few days in Rome and Paris. I was picked up from the Leonardo da Vinci Airport and shown around in a limousine with Doug and Joel. It was perfect. The next day, after staying at a superior hotel in a beautiful room on my own, we flew on to Paris. I love Paris and had been there many times before, even working on a film there at one point.

A newcomer to films was making his début at that time and Doug introduced me to him when we visited the Paris studios. It was Woody Allen. Doug said he was on his way to becoming a famous actor and director. He was right, of course, but I found Allen's nebbish Jewish mannerisms extremely irritating. At the time I couldn't believe he would make it in the film industry. How wrong I was!

As Doug and I were heading down the corridor, we walked past the bar and Doug turned to me and said, "Did you see Elizabeth Taylor sitting at the bar?" I didn't so backtracked to the entrance and looked in. There she was, one of the most famous actresses of her age. I was aghast as she looked so fat and old, and she was slumped over the bar. To be fair she had been in bad health for years and had still given great performances in films like *Who's Afraid of Virginia Woolf* and famously as *Cleopatra*. It was sad to see her like that.

During this time my marriage was not going well. Probably my husband and I were just developing differently.. I needed lots of affection and he was not giving me any. The sexual side of our relationship was frustrating for me and always left him satisfied but with me in tears. In the end I refused to have physical contact with him. I tried to talk to him about our difficulties, but he didn't want to know and was not prepared to work through them with me. It reached the stage where I told him I wanted to leave him, and I consulted a solicitor.

I have always written poems and always wanted to sing. In the 1960s the guitar was the 'in' instrument to accompany singing, and so in 1964 I joined an evening class at Middlesex Polytechnic in Hendon to learn to play the guitar in order to put my poems to music.

There I met a young non-Jewish man called George Rooker, who had recently come back from Australia where he had been living for four years. He and his family (which included three sisters and a brother) had all emigrated to Australia as '£10 poms' in the 1950s. He played the classical guitar beautifully and he was a bachelor. We got talking, but he was shy and it took months for him to ask me to have a coffee with him. I told him I was married and had two children. Our teacher, the renowned banjo player Al Jeffery, told him to beware of me for that reason. George had studied engineering at Middlesex Poly before he went to Australia and had learnt classical guitar under Al Jeffery's tuition at that time. Al was married to the actress Rita Webb and later, when we were invited to their Notting Hill Gate home for tea, we were entertained by the diminutive Rita who endearingly addressed her husband as 'Jeffee' – with her voice rising on the 'ee'.

In spite of Al's reservations he was happy to give us lifts in his VW Beetle. One evening he dropped us off in Willesden Green and George and I had our first coffee together in a café there. I asked him to give me extra lessons on the guitar and we were soon meeting as often as we could. I used to go over to George's place and there I met his Swiss-born mother. She spoke English with a Swiss-German accent, so I felt quite at home with her. She was welcoming and seemed to enjoy my company. By 1966, George and I decided we should be together permanently after I divorced my husband.

George went to see my husband in early 1966, before I left him, to try to sort things out amicably, but my husband wasn't having any of it and promised to make things as difficult as possible for George and me. He added that he would also drag my father's name through the mud.

George then went to see my father. This was excruciatingly hard for him, a non-Jewish man going to see my rabbi father. George knew nothing about my religion. He had innocently fallen in love with me and now wanted to do the right thing and explain things to my father. Dad had his position to protect, however, and at that time believed he should have nothing to do with George.

My father had probably been relieved when I had married a Jewish man. After all, I had mixed with more non-Jewish friends throughout my career than Jewish ones. I once told him that I was unhappy with Globby, but he simply said that I had made my bed and would now have to lie in it. This did not sit well with me; I was never going to stay in an unhappy marriage, not even for Dad. I am a patient person, as befits a Taurus-born child, but when that patience is exhausted, then the bull charges. I had fallen in love with George and nothing was going to stop me marrying him when I was free. This was the 1960s and it was not common for Jews to 'marry out'. Now my father was confronted with the prospect of a Gentile son-in-law. He worried what his congregants and colleagues would say. So, on the one hand, we had no support from my parents and, on the other, a bitter and vindictive husband to contend with.

I used to take the children on Friday nights to my parents for the Sabbath meal and spend the evening with them. This was while I was separated from my husband and George took us to the house and dropped us off. He was not welcome in my parents' home, but in spite of this, he waited patiently all evening outside the house and took us back home at the end, not having had any supper. It was all very sad and I hated the situation, but was not prepared to lose my relationship with my mum and dad, or the bond between them and my children. Years later the situation did improve, but at that time it was very hard. George had never known his own father and Dad's rejection was another blow to him.

This time felt very schizophrenic to me. On 9th February 1966 I was working on a film called *Modesty Blaise* at Shepperton Studios and the next day my husband went to a business toy fair in Nuremburg, Germany.

Two days later I was working on a film called *Run Johnny Run* and the next day, on 12th February, I left the marital home with the children. George and his brother Richard helped us to move with a hired van. I took one or two items of furniture with me and some other pieces that I had bought.

I rented a flat near my old school in Elgin Avenue in Maida Vale. Our au pair Sheila, a lovely person, came with me and continued to help with the children and the flat. She stayed a few more months before leaving, but we stayed in touch.

I engaged some first-rate girls and a few odd ones. After one Norwegian girl had left I found that she hadn't been taking the empty milk bottles outside, but instead had been hoarding them beneath her bed! Another would spend time standing on her head because she said it would reduce the size of her nose.

Eventually, I was put in touch with a German girl called Rosemarie who was with a family in Edgware. She was not happy with them and after interviewing her, I invited her to join me and the children. Rosemarie loved us and became a real part of the family. She stayed a full year before she returned home to Stuttgart to marry her boyfriend Detlev.

Many years later George and I stayed with her when we took 20-year-old Darrell with us and drove in our motor van to Switzerland. We have remained good friends and we meet up whenever we are in Germany. She proved to be a helpful character witness on our behalf when Darrell, as an adult, made astonishing allegations of childhood cruelty against me and George. This was at a time when I was trying to have contact with my grandchildren and I describe this sorry episode later in the book.

In 1966 I was not in good health. The emotional strain was getting to me and I felt ill a lot of the time. I really thought when I married Globby that it would be a good marriage. We were both German born and Jewish, came from middle-class backgrounds and on paper we were ideally suited. But he was closed in and could not open up and tell me his thoughts and feelings, so I felt isolated from him. He could not show me the warmth and affection I craved, nor the physical expression of love and so I was hurt and frustrated. My feelings on leaving the marital home were confused. I hated the idea that my marriage was over, that I was taking the children away from their father, but I also felt relieved that I was making a new life with a man who truly loved me and with whom I had a solid friendship as well as a loving relationship.

I hoped that Globby would come and visit the children as soon as he came back from his trip. I left a note to say where I was and that he should phone me when he got back. He did so and I asked him to come over and see the children. At first he refused, saying he wouldn't visit me in my new home. I pointed out that if he thought that would be punishing me, he would only be hurting the children by not coming over, so eventually he relented and did come to see them.

At this time I had little idea of the consequences the divorce would have on my future life. It would lead me into a profession I had never even dreamt about.

George had rented a room near the flat I had moved into with the children in Maida Vale. From then onwards the painful and protracted divorce proceedings began.

CHAPTER 9
BATTLE IN THE HIGH COURT, PART 1

WARNING: The reader might find this and the next chapter heavy going. This is because it describes, in detail, my harrowing eight years in the High Courts. The experience was significant because it would change the whole course of my life.

My husband commenced divorce proceedings in the High Court of Justice Probate, Divorce and Admiralty Division in July 1966. The High Court of Justice in the Strand is a huge imposing Gothic-style building which was designed expressly with the purpose of intimidating the ordinary man in the street. If the reader thinks of Hogwarts School in Harry Potter, they may get the appropriate feel of what the High Court is like. Proceedings in the High Court usually involve not just a solicitor, but also barristers. This is an expensive business and my husband knew that I had hardly any money. He could have begun proceedings in a lower, local court which would not only have been more suitable but much less costly.

The solicitor I saw before I met George had told me to leave the marital home, which I did. It would prove to be incredibly bad advice.

In his petition for divorce, my husband had cited 'overfriendliness with other men' and listed Joel Spector, Douglas Fairbanks Jr., Huntington Hartford (the American millionaire heir to the A&P supermarket fortune, businessman, philanthropist, filmmaker, and art collector) and Rabbi Lionel Blue. Naming Lionel was comically absurd as he was not interested in women although we were then, and still are, good friends. I have never understood what was meant by 'overfriendliness'. This absurdity cast doubt over the other names as well, as indeed they were all just friends. In the acting profession everyone is a 'luvvie' or a 'darling'. This means nothing at all and superficial demonstrations of affection are the norm. To name these people in a divorce petition was just ridiculous.

Although the actual divorce hearing did not start until 30th October 1967, my husband was already making applications to the Court in August 1966 to wrest the children from me. There had been some unnecessary unpleasantness and altercations when he came to my flat for his access visits. I was, at the time, willing to give him the fullest access every evening. However, instead of cooperating sensibly he took advantage of the situation and was abusive and threatening. He reaffirmed his intention to drag me through the courts and said he would take the children from me and called me a bitch and a prostitute. This was becoming increasingly upsetting and I hoped that things would improve if precise times for visits were set down by the court. By the time of the divorce hearing my soon-to-be ex had tried on three separate occasions to obtain custody of Kerry and Darrell, but failed each time. These preliminary hearings were before. We had been able to obtain legal aid and were represented by a QC, a junior barrister and solicitors.

An agreed settlement had been hammered out, and the uncontested divorce was granted on the basis of my adultery with George. Significantly, no adultery was alleged prior to me leaving my husband. In accordance with the ancient, feudal practices still existing at that time, George, as the guilty co-respondent, had to pay damages to my former husband, for loss of conjugal rights, to the sum of £70 and 10 shillings, by 12 equal monthly instalments. My husband agreed that, in return for my allowing him an uncontested divorce, I was to have care and control of the children, meaning they would live with me. Thankfully, precise times for access were included in the court order which I thought would alleviate any visiting problems. The initial advice I had been given by my solicitors to leave the matrimonial home proved detrimental because, by way of settlement, I received much less than my proper share of the value of the house which I had vacated, even though my parents had contributed to it financially.

On 31st January 1968 the divorce was made final and absolute and I hoped that the disagreeable events and memories of the litigation would recede into the past. I expected my ex-husband to stick to the terms of the agreed settlement.

I was wrong.

Later that same year he issued a summons to vary the order regarding care and control, by taking it away from me. We were back in court again. This time he was making allegations that the children were living in an unsatisfactory atmosphere and they should be removed from the influence of George. This was based on the fact that George and I were now living together, but were not married. My ex also complained about the lack of accommodation in the flat whereby the children did not have separate bedrooms. He was making nasty insinuations regarding the safety and welfare of the children. He asked that the court should order the children to live with him.

The next hearing was set down for 28th October 1968 and by then we had new solicitors.

We had an ace up our sleeve for the day of the hearing. In fact, we had two aces.

Three days earlier, on Friday 25th October, we had got married and over the next two days we moved into a huge 16-roomed house in West Hampstead. Not only were we now a respectable, legal couple, we had a house so big the children could have a whole suite of rooms each. The marriage took place at the Paddington Register Office on the Harrow Road. One of the witnesses was Rabbi Hugo Gryn. He was the associate rabbi at my father's synagogue and had become a friend to me and George. After the ceremony we had a small gathering in the garden of our flat to celebrate, before changing into clothes more suitable for moving home. Our honeymoon would have to wait!

From now on I would be known to the court as Mrs Rooker. At the hearing, the judge made an order that a welfare officer's report be obtained in respect of the children, which we welcomed. The Court Welfare Officer, Mr B., met with all parties, including the children, separately. In the report dated 20th February 1969 it showed that my ex-husband was still making outrageous allegations about my fitness to be a mother. However, as we expected, the report concluded that the children were happy living with me and George and showed 'none of the problems that are often associated with children from broken homes'. We were amused by the report's reference to us living 'in a very large house in St John's Wood' where 'the accommodation is spacious, well furnished and clean and comfortable'. Thank goodness that, in December 1970, my ex-husband's application for care and control was dismissed by Mr Justice Latey.

A series of protracted meetings and hearings before a registrar had taken place regarding maintenance for the children but, by the end of them, I was no better off than before. We were becoming increasingly frustrated with our lawyers. I knew what really happened about the matters being dealt with in the court, but realised that the facts were not being properly presented. We thought we could do a better job ourselves, or at least no worse. We dismissed our solicitors in July 1971 and after that appeared as *litigants in person*. George had been researching in the library and became proficient in preparing documents and understanding the court and legal procedures. Because of my professional acting training and experience I had the confidence to present our case in front of a judge. I felt that we would make a good team, should it become necessary to go to court again.

My ex-husband stopped coming to collect the children for his access rights after disagreements with them. The last occurred over the Easter weekend in 1971. We hoped that this meant he had finally accepted that life had changed, and that the disturbance to our family unit had now ceased.

Consequently, nothing prepared us for the next bombshell. One day in September 1972, 18 months after we had thought it was all over, our front door bell rang. On opening it I was served with an official legal document. The single sheet of paper was an application to the High Court, by my ex-husband, for an order that I be committed for an alleged failure to comply with the existing court order regarding access. We were shocked and dumbfounded. My ex-husband was now asking the court to send me to prison, because that is what being 'committed' means.

On 4th October 1972 we appeared again at the High Courts of Justice, but now for the first time it was in front of The Right Honourable, The President Sir George Gillespie Baker.

We were already familiar with the sombre buildings in the Strand, but knew nothing about the hierarchy of the courts. We had appeared before various judges but now found that our case was to be heard by the president of the Family Division. He is the most senior judge of the Family Division of the High Court and only deals with the most contentious cases. Once again we were entering unknown territory and were feeling apprehensive. But we had knowledge of one important thing from our previous experiences in the courts; the proceedings were recorded and transcripts of every spoken word were available – subject to payment of course. As we would henceforth be conducting our case in person, we decided it would be prudent to obtain transcripts. We could not foresee how useful they would become.

The president sits in his own court in an elevated position and wears a red robe. We became aware that there was another new figure in the court on that day. This was the tipstaff. We quickly discovered that he was the

High Court's law enforcement officer and acts on the judge's directions when someone is committed. He would be escorting me to prison if my ex-husband's application was successful. I had no desire to see the inside of Her Majesty's Prison Holloway and I was terrified, but also very angry at the lengths to which my ex-husband was prepared to go, in order to achieve his ends. Committal hearings are not in chambers but in open court and the words quoted here are taken from official transcripts of the proceedings.

As litigants in person, George and I took our place on the front bench where the QCs sit. My ex was sitting three rows back behind his solicitors – in the back of the stalls as it were. It was a bit like a theatre and I was ready to play my part.

My ex-husband's counsel, Mr C., opened the proceedings with the traditional phrase 'May it please your Lordship', and stated that it was an application to commit me for being in breach of an order which laid down specific access. To my surprise he then went into quick reverse and explained that what his client wants is access and not to commit his former wife to prison for contempt. He continued with a feeble explanation that those instructing him were informed that the appropriate way of going about it was to apply for committal. The informed reader will know that the way things work in court is that barristers get instructions from the solicitors and the solicitors gets instructions from the client. In the matter that was unfolding before his Lordship there was already a strong whiff of passing the buck.

The president gave my ex-husband's counsel enough time before commenting that the way they had gone about it 'seems a heavy hammer to take'. Counsel grovelled and said that he, with respect, agreed. He grovelled even more and said, "It would not do anybody any good in this case, I anticipate, for me to press for the respondent's committal to prison." I was relieved that it now seemed unlikely I would go to prison, but I was incensed at the worry and sleepless nights I had endured up to that point. Nobody had the courtesy to advise me that it was not their intention to imprison me. I have never, to this day, received an apology for the trauma we, as a family, had been put through.

The president was not going to let Mr C. wriggle out of it that easily and wondered who had given the information that it had to be done by committal. It was our first day in court representing ourselves and my ex's legal team were being probed about their inappropriate methods. I found this to be an unexpected and interesting development.

When it was my turn to speak I explained that it was my belief that my ex was a vexatious litigant and was repeatedly bringing us back to court for no good reason. I said that I wanted to cross-examine him on all the claims and allegations he had made in his various affidavits and statements. The president said that from what I was saying it seemed necessary to have a welfare officer's report, the last one having been prepared almost four years earlier.

Exchanges went back and forth, but something was still bothering the president. Addressing my ex's counsel he said: "... I must ask you again, who was it who told you that you must take out a summons in this form, because right from the start this seemed very odd to me."

Mr C. fumbled and said, "Apparently, my Lord, it was in a room, which is unknown to me, which used to be Room 30, I understand – the old Room 30, I am reminded."

Mr C. was now squirming and went on to say that the original draft of the summons, before it was amended, showed what his client really wanted. The president was not impressed and quoted from the document in his hand which plainly stated that the respondent (me) should be committed. This reaffirmed my belief that it was better to appear in person than to rely on 'learned counsel' who are ill prepared, not in possession of all the facts or often simply not up to it.

Finally, the president had heard enough and he pointed out that he had a full list that day and there was no time to go into all the contentious issues in this case. He made an order that the summons be amended to delete the application for committal and substitute an application for directions. To our surprise the president went further than we had anticipated by not allowing my ex-husband to have any access to the children until further notice. He also ordered the High Court Welfare Officer to prepare a new report. Mr C. requested that a different welfare officer be used, and I agreed. The president concurred and said that he wanted 'one of our own welfare officers'. The hearing was adjourned. My first day in court, in person, was over. I was flying solo and it had not gone too badly.

I wondered how long my ex-husband would go on with his litigation. He too had got remarried by this time, and I could not understand why he did not just get on with building a new life for himself and his new wife. He had been given generous access rights to his children but had failed to exercise them fully. He had blown it. They were now 14 and 11 and had their own issues with him because of his attitude towards them. It seemed obvious that the sole purpose of his continuing litigation was to punish me and George in some way.

Something extraordinarily nice happened after the committal hearing. We made friends with the tipstaff, who was now no longer a fearful figure. He was a short gentleman dressed in a decorated uniform and he invited us back to his small office in the bowels of the court. We were allowed to examine the physical tipstaff which is a small hollow baton topped with a silver crown in which the warrant of arrest is stored. (The office of tipstaff dates from the fourteenth century and the wooden tipstaff was the origin for the much later police truncheon.) He introduced us to the two volumes of rules and regulations which govern the practices of the High Courts. These are known informally as the *White Books*. Amazingly he said we could borrow them, which we did, and they helped us greatly in preparation of our case. We were discovering that the High Courts had a human face – and it would not be for the last time.

We had no qualms about another welfare officer investigating our family life as long as it would help bring an end to the litigation. The report by the Court Welfare Officer Mrs S. was ready in December 1972. Helpfully for us, it stated that because of my ex-husband's disruptive behaviour with his children, they no longer wished to see him again. The report also reiterated the fact that they were happy living with me and George. But we were not satisfied with some of the things in the report which distorted what the children had told her during their interview and misconstrued some other matters. For this reason I wanted to cross-examine the welfare officer. This would be a first for me and also, I would swiftly learn, a first for the court.

The hearing recommenced on 15th February 1973. Mr C., the former counsel, was not there – perhaps he had had enough. My ex-husband was now represented by Mr H.

I addressed the president and stated that I wanted to start by asking the welfare officer some questions. The president was initially reluctant to allow me this concession. He said that it was not his practice to allow cross-examination of the court welfare officer because, in one sense, she was the 'eyes and ears of the court'. He asked Mrs S. if she would mind and she said she had 'no objection whatsoever'.

During the morning examination, I managed to extract the admission from Mrs S. that she had mixed up words said by my ex and me and wrongly attributed them. I also obtained clarification on other matters and established that the report was not impartial. When I had finished, the president said to me, and here I have the invaluable benefit of the transcript for authentication: "I thought you had established all the points in what I might say was an almost brilliant cross-examination." I thanked him. Perhaps he was grateful that I had shown that the court's 'eyes and ears' had some imperfections. It was my wish that the president should meet my children himself as I was fed up with the welfare reports.

My first attempt at cross-examination, thinking on my feet, had been quite productive. This was not acting; it was real. There was still a long way to go, but we had proved our point; none of the significant discrepancies would have even been noticed let alone exposed, if we had used a solicitor/barrister team to represent us.

We had earlier issued a writ of subpoena for Mrs X., a house mistress at Kerry's school, to appear at court. I wanted her to produce a particular document. It was central to my belief that my ex-husband had gone behind our backs and caused mischief at Kerry's school to her detriment. Because of this, Kerry had to change schools and lost all her friends. This did nothing to help her relationship with her father.

After the lunch break my ex-husband was sworn in so that I could start my cross-examination of him. I had waited a long time for this opportunity. I had barely started asking him my first question based on his affidavit when the president interrupted me. He instructed Mr H. to give his client a copy of the affidavit. Mr H. was flummoxed. "My Lord, I am extremely embarrassed to say that I cannot. My Lord, I am loath to hand up my own copy because, naturally, there are comments on it." The president said that he would hand his copy over. Oops, Mr H. had not prepared well!

Firstly, I sought to establish why my ex-husband had wanted the children to stay with him when he was going off to work. Then I moved onto the crucial matter – the matter that had so concerned the president back in October: had my ex instructed his solicitors to ask for me to be committed? When I put that question to my ex he replied "no". When I asked, "Did they tell you that they would bring such a summons?" he again answered "no".

My ex then blithely commented, "It is quite irrelevant." I pressed him again and he protested saying that he did not look at the wording on every document. He said, "I trust my solicitors."

I continued, "In other words, your solicitors act for you without your knowledge. Is that correct?"

He disagreed; he said it was "an error". The president intervened to try to achieve some clarity. My ex then admitted, "I knew a summons had been issued but not for committal."

I then put to my ex the contradictions which existed between the explanation given by two of his own counsels. On 4th October 1972, Mr C. had given a version of events which referred to a Room 30. (My ex and I were both present at that hearing and heard that version.) But a different account was given by his counsel Mr J. who attended Court on 17th January 1973 in front of a registrar Mr G., when my ex had *not* been present. It was this latter version which appeared in my ex's affidavit; the version when he did not attend court. Most odd. It was beyond my ex-husband's grasp who said: "I am sorry. I just do not follow the question. It has become meaningless." I tried another approach, but my ex could still not comprehend the issue.

I turned to the president and asked, "My Lord, do you understand what I am saying?"

He replied, "Perfectly." Just a single word, but it meant so much. It was the president whom I had to win over, not my ex.

Amongst a lot of other topics I managed to expose my ex-husband's hypocrisy when he claimed that the children were in 'moral danger' living with us when George and I were not married. He had to admit it was true that his own stepmother lived with a Mr K.W. when they were not married.

The president chided me at one point when he thought my questioning was drifting. But he went on to say, "You are a very clever woman and you are a very able woman." The compliment was nice, but more gratifying was having it said by an experienced legal mind in front of my ex-husband who used to berate me by telling me I was too stupid to learn to play chess.

The president did not want to rule out completely any possibility of my ex seeing the children again, so he raised the idea of involving the Official Solicitor to represent the children. However, he said he would not do that until he had met both children. I was pleased he was minded to see the children personally, as that was my hope after the last welfare report.

But here was somebody new – the Official Solicitor. Who was he?

Mr H. said that this was a case where the children had been indoctrinated against their father. The president agreed that even if the indoctrination was not deliberate, my having a chip on my shoulder (with regard to my ex) would have rubbed off on the children. But he also said to Mr H., "And unfortunately, of course, your man has been, perhaps putting it neutrally, not very clever in April of 1971." So the president was remaining impartial.

Now it was my turn to go into the witness box so that I could be sworn in to give my own evidence. I stated that I intended to show that my ex was not a fit person to have custody of the children. I would also show that he was a vexatious litigant in that he was harassing me by repeatedly taking me to court. I recounted everything that had happened since his court applications began years before. When I was finished it was my turn to be cross-examined by Mr H. but nothing was achieved by him.

I have spared the reader much of the minutiae of evidence that was ploughed through during the hearing. The transcript of that day alone runs to 63 pages. Instead I can do no better than to give the reader a feel for the days in court by quoting a few of the exchanges. They are verbatim and, therefore, cannot be challenged, although looking back on it now it all seems like a strange dream.

The president was not above making some esoteric amusing asides as the following demonstrates.

The president: "Wait a minute. Mr H. has given me a wrong date or I have misheard him."

Mr H: "My Lord, I am quite certain I gave your Lordship the wrong date because I have got it down wrong in my summary."

The president: "Yes. I hope nobody suggests there is anything ulterior in that."

I'm sure I saw the twinkle in his eye.

The hearing was adjourned at the end of the first day to resume again at 10.30 am the following morning. On the next day I was re-called to continue the cross-examination, but nothing was accomplished by way of resolving any of the outstanding issues. The children had accompanied us to court that morning and were being looked after by a family friend. The president instructed the usher to bring the children in to him, then retired to his chambers where he would see them for 40 minutes.

After an adjournment the president returned and gave his judgment. In it he summarised the case. Referring to the summons for committal he decided it was a genuine misunderstanding. But he went on: "So the Summons was served seeking committal. Nothing could have been more unfortunate. That certainly was like the proverbial red rag to the bull, to the mother." (He could not know that my astrological sign was Taurus.) He dismissed the idea of my ex being a vexatious litigant and also acquitted him of any conspiracy against me. He went on to say: "I have seen Mrs Rooker, who has conducted this case with consummate skill and made all the points that she wanted to make clearly and vigorously." Referring to my suggestion that the welfare officer's report was biased he said: "There were certain things in the report which Mrs Rooker brought out in cross-examination and, if I may say so, brought out brilliantly. It was very well done."

Regarding the children, whom he had interviewed earlier, he said: "This case concerns two delightful youngsters... I have seen the children. I had a long talk to them. Indeed, I think we got to know each other quite well... I have no doubt from what Darrell has told me that he gets on famously with Mr Rooker. There is no doubt about that at all... I do not think there can be any doubt from the way he talked to me that they are great friends. They play together, and so on."

It was good to know that he had made up his own mind about the children's characters and their positive relationship with their stepfather George. The president could have ended the case then and there – and in retrospect, as I was to find out much later, he wished he had.

Instead he said: "Now what is to be done? It seems to me first that it would be unreal to leave custody with the father. At the same time I am not going to let Mrs Rooker (and I am quite certain she will realise what is behind all this) go away from here thinking she has scored a great victory and give her custody. I am going to leave custody, as it were, in the Court. Now in my view, the interests of the children require, setting aside all the feelings of both parents, that they ought to continue to see their father. Quite clearly, there cannot be anything like the access there was before. That simply would not work. The only thing that is possible (one has to be conscious all the time of reality) is that they should start seeing their father once a month, for at the outside a couple of hours, or even an hour. I will hear what you think about that in a minute."

I groaned inwardly. I had mustered all my persuasive skills to explain to the court that the relationship between the children and their father was over. We were now a happy family. The only disruption to it was caused by my ex for his own perverse reasons and now the president was going to prolong the agony for us.

He wanted the parties to arrange for the children to meet with their father and if that did not work, he would bring in the Official Solicitor as *guardian ad litem*. He invited Mr H. to make some proposals. There was a long discussion while he took instructions and then he inadvisably suggested that Mrs S., the welfare officer, might be available for supervision of the meetings. That did not go down well with the president: "I cannot have welfare officers supervising on a Saturday. It just is not possible."

I rose and made a more sensible suggestion (whispered to me by George) that a rabbi who was neutral to both sides, would be best. This was accepted and my ex proposed (the late) Rabbi Michael Leigh whom I knew well. Dates and times were then discussed and the president concluded the hearing by saying he would make no order for costs of any kind.

His final words, addressed to Mr H. were: "Does the gentleman behind you know anything about the Summons?" The 'gentleman' in question was my ex's solicitor. In spite of the president letting them off the hook, as I quoted earlier, he was not done with the matter quite yet. Someone was about to face the music. Unfortunately, the court tape ends at this point.

We had been under a lot of pressure and were sorely in need of a few days respite, so before the court adjourned I had obtained the president's consent for me and George to take the children to France for a 'petite' holiday. A week later we crossed the channel by hovercraft from Ramsgate to Calais and then drove on to Paris via Amiens and Arras in our little Mini. We spent four lovely days together as a family and Kerry and Darrell were excited as we showed them all the sights including the Arc de Triomphe, the Eiffel Tower and took them on a cruise on the River Seine.

On our return we complied with the arrangements which had been made for the children to meet with their father under supervision. It turned out to be a disaster. The first date was 3rd March 1973 at the rabbi's home. My ex left before his allotted hour was up. The children were nervous and stressed before and after the meeting. When the rabbi later spoke to the children to arrange the next month's meeting they told him they did not want to see their father again. No attempt was made to arrange more meetings.

Wedding Day with George's Mum, a guest, Sheppie,
Darrell and Kerry, 1968

CHAPTER 10
BATTLE IN THE HIGH COURT, PART 2

We did not want things to drift for months again; we had had enough. We wanted some certainty to our lives, so we took the case back to court in May 1973 by way of a summons. Our application asked that because the petitioner (my ex-husband) had failed to exercise his access, that I be granted custody with no access by my ex. But we had made a procedural error and failed to file an affidavit with the summons. We were in a hurry and this slip-up was to cause us some difficulty.

When I gave my opening address I immediately made it clear to the president that I would go to any lengths to oppose all further attempts to make the children see their father under any circumstances. I said that I did not want their happy dispositions and mental health threatened. I wanted the court to make a final order in the case today. Because the president had previously speculated that if my ex-husband could not see the children, he might stop paying maintenance, I made a few points about that. I went into some detail to show that my ex was a director of more than one company and based on the remuneration he received, could afford to pay much more than the meagre amount of maintenance I was receiving at that time for the children.

When it was Mr H's turn he indicated that Rabbi Leigh was in court and "will be in a position to assist your Lordship as to what he saw take place on this last occasion". This referred to the meeting of my ex with the children. Mr H. then said he was "very distressed to hear this lady use the words 'any lengths' to stop the children ever seeing their father again. My Lord, I would like to ask her what she means by that." He may have thought I had been too reckless and would fall foul of the president.

Because I had failed to prepare an affidavit I was sworn in again so that I could be cross-examined by Mr H. He wanted to know why, if I was so concerned about the children's distress, I had not issued the summons earlier. He asked about Kerry changing school and I explained that it was necessary because of the way his client had interfered at her previous school. We sparred for a bit, but he got nowhere so he moved on to what he thought would be a more successful line of questioning.

He asked, "When you made your opening remarks to his Lordship you said that you would be prepared to go to any lengths to ensure these children do not see their father again?"

I replied, "Yes. And you must bear in mind my motive, which is purely the protection of my children."

He pressed further, "By that do I take it you have no intention of obeying an order of the Court if access were ordered?"

"Absolutely," I replied. This was a direct challenge to the president. I was risking being in contempt of court; would the tipstaff be called back?

Mr H. asked, "And if necessary you would take the children abroad and keep them abroad so that your former husband could never see them?"

This was just ridiculous, so I said, "I would never envisage anything. Anything that you say is pure conjecture. I would hope that I would not need to be in contempt of this court."

The president intervened, "Is there anything you wish to add?"

I said, "My Lord, I am a law-abiding citizen, but I am also a loving mother and at the moment the two do not seem compatible. I hope that they will be." I then withdrew from the witness box.

Rabbi Leigh was then sworn in and he was examined by Mr H. The questions and answers confirmed the fact that the meeting between my ex and the children had not gone well. When the rabbi phoned the next month to arrange a further meeting, both children told him independently that they did not want to see their father again. I was offered the opportunity to question the rabbi but I declined. I could see no point; it had been clearly established that the children's relationship with their father had been damaged beyond repair.

My ex was examined next and the president asked if he had any views to improve or resolve the situation. He could come up with only one proposal: "It might be possible – but again this could hurt the children and I do not want to do this – to send the children to boarding school, so that at least they do not have what I consider a bad influence on them in their daily lives. But this really does not solve the pressures they have been under, and are continually under, because this is not something that just happens before meetings with me."

The children were well cared for and living as normal a life as possible with a loving mother and stepfather. Their lives were full of friends, activities, holidays and were enriched by the regular contact with their grandparents. If my ex had accepted that his marriage to me had ended and could have conducted himself in a civil way, he could have been part of it. There are plenty of examples of divorced couples getting on perfectly well together. Instead, through his own actions, he had destroyed any possibility of being involved in our lives.

The president responded: "Well, there is no solution when the children are got into this stage and I have to remind myself that I saw these children on the last occasion. But there is one course which is open; it is the last resort course. That is, to ask the Official Solicitor to come in and act as guardian for these children for the litigation and the whole matter can be investigated and sometimes that results in a little sense in the situation. What are your views? Well, I had better ask your Counsel. You had perhaps better talk to him about it, but that is the only possibility I can see at the present time. Mr H., I cannot see any course here other than that. I will give Mrs Rooker, of course, the opportunity to cross-examine and say what she wants to say about this. But it seems to me this is the last resort case. It is no good ordering further access because in the end it will simply mean Mrs Rooker going to prison by the look of things just now and it has gone too far with the children."

I was comforted by the president's concern that I might end up in Holloway, but I was discouraged by his intention to prolong the case by introducing the Official Solicitor.

In the intervening time since this name had been first mentioned we had done some research. The Office of the Official Solicitor (OS) is a part of the Ministry of Justice and acts for people who are unable to represent themselves. In our case he would act for the children who were being made party to the proceedings. I was not happy that they were being dragged into the case when I was doing all I could to protect them and let them get on with a normal life. The then holder of the office, Mr Norman Turner, had been involved in the Pentonville Five case, when there was a legal stalemate between the TUC and the government. Five shop stewards from the Dockers' Union had been imprisoned on a charge of contempt. Well maybe he was just the man to bring some sense to our case. Our hopes were not to be fulfilled.

Mr H. then gave his views on the available options: "There only remain two. One is perhaps some independent representation with the possibility of a change of atmosphere in the future, if recommended by the Official Solicitor, such as Mr Jondorf has said: boarding school – something of that nature. Apart from that, there remains only the very, very last resort of no access ever to..."

The president took over: "Well, either Mr Jondorf throws in his hand, or we make an order which, unless this lady changes her ideas, will ultimately result in her going to prison for contempt. The only other course is the Official Solicitor."

After some further exchanges in which I, reluctantly, agreed with the introduction of the OS, Mr H. came back: "My Lord, as I suspected, Mr Jondorf is anxious to try any avenue that is still open before all doors are closed." Well yes, he would say that wouldn't he? As long as it kept up the pressure on us, I thought.

The president gave his judgment: "I saw the children on the last occasion. I am not going to say any more than that I am extremely disappointed that this endeavour to get access working has completely failed, and, of course, the inference is there to be drawn as to why it has failed. I could, I suppose, say that there is to be access and if Mrs Rooker does not indicate to the children that they must obey the order of the Court, then she is going to be in trouble. However, against all the background of this case I am not going to take that course for it may be that the situation is now hopeless and the Official Solicitor will so report. I will, however, repeat what I think I said on the last occasion that, as so often happens in cases of this kind, Mrs Rooker may be storing up a great deal of trouble for herself when the children are a little older and begin to realise that father is not as bad as he has been painted. I am going to refer this matter to the Official Solicitor and invite him, if he thinks it is possible, to represent the children."

His final closing remarks were: "Now I am told there is an embryo bomb scare but not sufficient to clear the building, so perhaps we had better adjourn for the moment. That concludes this matter."

So there it was: I was not going to prison; the case was not at an end. It would drag on for almost another two years. The president was right about trouble in the future, but it was not when the children were just a little older. It was many years later that my adult son would get back in touch with his father – and resurrect all the old resentments and cause a new period of anguish. But more of that in a later chapter. For now I walked out of court, still a free woman. It had been a strange day. In the morning I challenged the president and afterwards had lunch in nearby Chancery Lane. At 5.00 pm I did a voice test in Dean Street and later went to a symposium with my mother. No lack of variety to complain about then!

In June 1973 the OS filed an *Acknowledgement of Service – Party other than spouse*. It formally stated that "I, the Official Solicitor to the Supreme Court of the Royal Courts of Justice, London, HEREBY CONSENT to be appointed and to act as *Guardian ad litem* of Kerry Lyn and Darrel Davrd the Infant Interveners in the matter." Unfortunately, they had managed to get Darrell's middle name, 'David', wrong. Not a good start.

It may be helpful for the reader to know that the phrase *guardian ad litem* literally means your 'guardian in the court'.

We felt that this case had been going on for far too long. George's career in engineering design had suffered. Frequent absence from work to attend court or prepare for hearings made sure he missed opportunities for promotion, although he managed to secure freelance work. But our experience in court had opened our eyes. There was nothing better than appearing in person to experience the daunting environment of the High Courts and learn how the system works. By all accounts I had done a good job, so far, and with George's meticulous care in preparing documents we had dealt with everything that was thrown at us. But winning is a different matter.

Another thought had entered my mind: why shouldn't I become a lawyer – a barrister? I would be able to help people like us – the innocent party. The thought became a reality and I decided to follow up on this aspiration. In September 1973 I took the first step by enrolling at Kilburn Polytechnic to study for two A-Levels.

Later, in 1973 we had received a letter from the OS saying he wanted his colleague Mrs B. to interview all parties to the case and asked us to indicate a convenient date for ourselves. Things now became even more difficult. There had already been two reports which indicated that the children were happy and well cared for and we thought the case, which had now been going on for seven years should have been wound up. If it was to go on, we wanted to make sure that there would be no more discrepancies, distortions, misquotations or 'mistakes' in the reports and other evidence, as happened previously. For that reason, not unreasonably we thought, we wanted the children's interviews to be recorded. I declined to be interviewed because, having appeared in court several times, the president was already familiar, perhaps over-familiar, with my views.

An exchange of several letters between us and the OS, and a meeting with Mrs B. at his offices, failed to solve the impasse. The OS wrote to us saying he would apply to the court to see if he should continue in his role as guardian or, alternatively, obtain specific directions as to the arrangements being made to interview the children. In October 1973 he produced his first report. He admitted that, in order to arrange to see Kerry (also called 'Terry' in the report), he had written to the wrong school; the one she had left at the beginning of the year. An easily rectified mistake, but the lack of professionalism that we were encountering did not impress us.

At the end of the two-day hearing which started on 9th November 1973, the president ordered that the OS continue in the case and see the children 'in such circumstance as he thinks best and proper'. We were ordered to pay the costs of that hearing, both for the OS and my ex. This unfair imposition would trigger another battle. The whole business had become a colossal burden; all we wanted was for the nightmare to stop. Our initial expectation of some common sense illuminating the situation regarding the children and their father had been naive. More and more officials were going through the motions of caring, but nobody truly did. For them all, at the end of the day, it was just another case. For us, it was our intimate family life and the children that we were anxious to protect.

On 4th December 1973 we went to see the OS at his offices to discuss the case. Mrs B. subsequently saw the children a week later in our home at Broadhurst Gardens. She had taken notes and these were sent to the children for them to verify their accuracy. Her report stated that the children were adamant that they did want to have anything further to do with their father. They said that he was a stranger to them and why would the judge make them see a total stranger? The report confirmed the close relationship they had with me and George whom they described as 'fantastic'.

In May 1974 the OS completed his second report. In the summer of that same year I took and passed my GCE A-Level exams. I then enrolled at Middlesex Polytechnic, where George and I had first met, to commence studying for my law degree, starting in September. My studies were quickly interrupted because on 9th October 1974 we were back in the President's Court once more. It was becoming crowded. Not only were the usual participants there, but now also the Official Solicitor and his counsel Mr F. were present. The children were nearly 16 and 13.

Mr F. opened with the usual introductions, then said: "There are four summonses presently before the Court, two restored summonses and two new summonses. I see the Associate shaking his head; possibly I have made a mistake in that respect." To err is human, but a mistake so soon in the proceedings! If the matters were not so important to us, it would be entertaining. In the legal world everything hangs on the precise meanings of words but we had learnt that carelessness and unpreparedness seemed to be the norm. Mr F. went through it all again, reminding the president of the long drawn out history.

A long discussion ensued about the Premium Bonds (worth all of £1,300) which had been purchased for the children by my parents. They were in the possession of their father, but should they be handed over and if so to whom? This was a minuscule matter, but it was apparently worthy of deep legalistic consideration and might even have to be decided by a higher legal authority.

Mr F.: "So far as one can tell, if, as in these proceedings, the Official Solicitor is opposed in the matrimonial jurisdiction as opposed to wardship jurisdiction, he seems possibly that he cannot hold a premium bond or at least render accounts and deal with them, unless your Lordship thought that this Court, and your Lordship sitting as a High Court Judge, has inherent Chancery jurisdiction and therefore it could be dealt with in that way. But, my Lord, the Official Solicitor is prepared to hold those premium bonds, if your Lordship thought right; and he would seek possibly directions from your Lordship as to whether or not the children would have to be made wards of court in this respect."

Was the learned counsel being paid according to the degree of obfuscation he could introduce into what was essentially a straightforward matter?

The president: "It seems a tremendous 'hammer' for a very little 'nut', does it not?"

Mr F.: "Yes, my Lord, it does."

The mere suggestion that the children should become wards of court over some premium bonds was indicative of how far the madness had gone. The discussion continued with details about who could or couldn't manage the bonds and Mr F. read great chunks from the reports. So much time was consumed that it was close to lunch time when the president invited me to speak. I responded: "My Lord, I see that we only have about six minutes left before luncheon, and as I wish to address you a little more lengthily than ten minutes on my summonses I respectfully submit you might like to adjourn until after lunch. I don't know how you feel about that."

The president: "I think that is not a bad idea. What do counsel feel? ... Very well – back at 2 o'clock." So the learned judge and I at least agreed on when it was time for lunch!

After the break, it was my turn. I wanted to show that perjury had been committed in court, by my ex and the teacher. If I could prove that, then the proper thing would be to roll-back the proceedings to that point and allow the president to re-think the judgments he had made. I was trying to persuade him to retrace his steps. In connection with costs, I argued that he had not been consistent in ordering costs against the parties. My ex had failed with his summons to commit me, but costs were not ordered against him. The only time we had successfully recovered costs in the proceedings, amounted to one pound and eight pennies. Yes, £1.08. We could only claim for expenses and not the considerable amount of time incurred in preparing for each hearing.

I then honed in on one particular item. In a bill of costs prepared by my ex-husband's solicitors which we had been ordered to pay, there was an item on page 3 for 'attending Mr Field to obtain from him details of children's schooling and relevant dates thereof'. We had checked up with Mr Field (the headmaster at Kerry's old school) and he sent us a letter assuring us that he had no recollection of being approached by my ex's solicitors and said that we were misinformed. I was submitting his letter as evidence.

Next, I turned to the effects that the president's ordering costs against us was having on us as a family, including the children. We were existing on a shoestring because of the disruptive effects the case had on our earning ability. I asked that the orders for costs be varied so that all parties bear their own costs.

I returned to the matter of perjury. It all revolved around one specific document: the original pupil entrance form. My ex-husband and Mrs X. (the house teacher) claimed that I had represented myself as having custody, when I clearly did not. Counsel for my ex had never tendered this crucial document in evidence. I reminded the president that, following my examination of them, he had acquitted my ex and Mrs X. of perjury. Indeed, he went even further and commended her. The positive views the president had of them had influenced his judgment against me. I explained, in great detail, the words that each had said about the form and reminded the president how 'incensed' my ex had been when he saw it. I submitted that in this light, all the rest of their evidence, which had been in generalities, should be doubted. I continued by reiterating the now contrary reasons for my ex going to court in October 1972. At that time he claimed it was over access, later he said it was because he was contacted by Kerry's teacher.

The president and Mr H. then discussed the premium bonds again at some length. When Mr H. eventually got around to my allegation of perjury he tried to confuse the issue by saying there were two forms, one of which was the school 'entrance form'. He said: "So, my Lord, if I may, without disrespect to the eloquence with which Mrs Rooker has put forward her argument..."

He was not allowed to finish. The president asked: "Has anybody got the form that was produced to me at the time that Mrs X. gave evidence, if there was such a form?" Mr H. said that no such form had been produced.

It was my turn to take the high ground. I said, "My Lord, I would just like to make one point on this. It was Mr H. who, at the hearing when he first had Mrs X. in the witness box, in fact led asking Mrs X. about this entrance form. And at a later date, when I was in the witness box, being cross-examined, Mr H. exhorted me that if I were referring to documents, they should be produced." I pressed for the form to be produced and said: "Is it a case that Mr H. failed to enquire about this form and check up on the petitioner's statement?"

The president then asked me: "Have you got a full transcript or only some pages of the transcript?" (Would I be foolish enough to have brought along just a few pages?)

I replied: "I have a full transcript, my Lord."

The President then commanded: "Now if everyone will sit down for a moment and let me look at this." It was a lovely moment – the class was to sit quietly while he studied it. But I regret to say it did not move the president to change his mind.

The president's judgment that day was a travesty. He ignored all my points; he reaffirmed the fact that we should pay the costs of the petitioner and the Official Solicitor, as previously ordered. He absolved Mrs X. of perjury – she had made a mistake. (Oh dear, so many mistakes in this case...) He dismissed my querying a false item on the petitioner's bill of costs, saying that it was not a matter for him. He refused to give me custody; it would remain with the court. He did, however, make one concession: for the hearing on that day, there would be no order as to costs. Maybe in his heart he knew we were in the right.

In September 1974 I sent a personal letter to the president. It referred to the transcript of the proceedings on 9th October. I drew his attention to three significant statements which were factually incorrect and requested that no reliance be place upon them. I received only a simple acknowledgment from his secretary.

It was not over yet. We were incensed by the order to pay what we considered were punitive costs, and wanted to bring home to the Official

Solicitor the consequences for the children, in whose interests he was supposed to be acting. We informed him that any financial burden placed on us, would be a burden on the children. To make the point we sent him postal orders amounting to £53.30, saying that we had borrowed the money from the children. We also summarised some of his prejudicial behaviour, for instance ignoring us outside the court but engaging in conversation with the other side.

The OS decided that he needed more instructions and so issued another summons which brought us back to court on 5th February 1975. I prepared a six-page affidavit for the occasion and issued a cross summons asking for reimbursement in lieu of costs and requesting the custody of the children. At the start of the hearing the president announced that he might have to make a statement in 'open court'. Did that he mean he would be recalling the tipstaff?

In his judgment, which turned out to be his last in this case, the president said my ex was a normal and reasonable man who had made a mistake. He criticised us for sending the letter to the OS saying the children had offered to pay his costs. If he had known about that in advance he would not have ordered the transfer of their premium bonds to us. (Well, we hadn't conceived of that idea before he penalised us with costs.) He quoted historical precedent by saying for over 200 years it has been settled law that a parent cannot use the children's money and quoted chapter and verse. He said he had the power to appoint a guardian of the children's estates, but will not make such an order. He offended George by saying he was 'in a permanent state of unemployment' and our penury was not a matter for him. He dismissed our summons and left the OS in place 'as a channel of communication'. The order stated that the sum of £53.50 paid by us with postal orders should remain in the Suspense Account of the Official Solicitor until further notice. For all we know, the money is still there gathering legal dust.

My view as to why my ex-husband had been continuously taking us to court was that he was motivated by revenge and wanted us to suffer financially. He knew we didn't have much money and reckoned that by going to the High Court, it would be much more stressful than if the matter was dealt with in a local court. Also, by continuously going back to court after the divorce, to try to reverse the 'care and control' it was a way of constantly getting at us. His bitterness remained and it was to affect us once again, after Darrell as an adult, renewed contact with his father.

The court proceedings were now more or less at an end. I am sure all the many lawyers involved had made a nice living from a case that had gone on for ten years. My ex-husband had almost succeeded in wresting the children from my care at one stage and gave us such a hard time that I never wanted to see him again. If he had accepted George's hand of friendship at the start and had not let me endure weeks of worry when I thought I would be committed, it could all have been so different. Ten whole years out of our lives was a great burden for us all. The whole purpose of the Family Courts is supposed to be for the benefit and well-being of children. However, in our case, it had caused a great deal of anguish and grief, with not one iota of benefit for the children.

Now that the proceedings were over I reverted to my maiden name for all purposes. George had no objections because he held the view that women should retain their own names after marriage.

Two weeks later George and I went on a hang-gliding course high on the South Downs behind Brighton. What better way to clear ones lungs from the musty air of the courts than by flinging oneself off a hilltop strapped to a metal frame covered by a bit of fabric? I went with an instructor, but George, adventurous as ever, went solo. Exhilaration!

Various letters continued to pass between us and the OS referring to school reports and requesting permission to take the children abroad on holiday. And then it petered out; the last letter was in August 1976, when Kerry was almost 18 and Darrell nearly 15.

CHAPTER 11
A KALEIDOSCOPIC LIFE

The High Courts of Justice and the neighbourhood of barristers' chambers called Middle Temple, are across the road from each other in the Strand.

Middle Temple is a warren of narrow lanes and picturesque, historic buildings. This is where every day, barristers clad in their traditional black gowns, clutching their wigs and legal briefs can be seen rushing to court. This was the most respected of hallowed environments – very proper, or so one thought. However, there was another side to all this which was unfolding at the same time as the court case and which made our life seem even more crazy.

Douglas Fairbanks Jr. had many friends in different walks of life and he introduced me and George to some of them. They used to have get-togethers in the apartments above the lawyers' chambers in Middle Temple, where interesting people came to have fun. The ambience of the 'Swinging Sixties' prevailed and we met household names on these occasions. It was a strange schizophrenic life we were leading. During the day I was working, often in Pinewood on the Bond films, or sometimes appearing in the High Court as a litigant and then occasionally, on some evenings, we saw an unexpected transformation to the legal precincts. We were poor as church mice, but mingling with the wealthy, the great and the good.

One of the most eminent people we met at these gatherings was Dr Will Sargant. He had been in charge of the Department of Psychological Medicine at St Thomas's Hospital and was then well known as the top man in British psychiatry. He was a charismatic figure and held controversial views on how to deal with mental illness.

Although highly respected, he was a bit of a maverick figure and promoted and defended the radical practice of lobotomy, long after it was considered an ineffective treatment. The procedure (also known as leucotomy) consists of cutting the connections to and from the prefrontal cortex, the anterior part of the frontal lobes of the brain. It was supposed to benefit mental disorders such as schizophrenia. By the early 1970s (when Will retired) the practice of lobotomy was generally in decline.

He also supported electroconvulsive therapy (ECT), formerly known as electroshock, for cases of severe depression. Many years later ECT would be used to treat one of my three sisters-in-law who lived in Australia. Georges's oldest sister had lost the ability to cope in her late '60s, after the loss of her husband. The hospital doctors proposed ECT treatment and her son and other members of the family agreed to this. George and I strongly opposed the use of what we considered was a barbaric method of dealing with depression. We have seen her many times since on our frequent visits to Australia and, although she suffers badly from memory loss, she seems to be happy and manages reasonably well.

In his book *Battle for the Mind* Sargant links shock treatment used in psychiatry with methods used in brainwashing and sudden religious conversion. He later examined the way that physical activities like dancing, music, drugs and sex can be used to create the mystical experience of union with God. He said that most of the spiritual states that he had studied were less God-given than manmade. He was convinced that man had created his gods in his own image.

Will Sargant was interested in psychotropic (mind-altering) drugs in the context of psychiatry at a time when recreational drug usage throughout British society was becoming increasingly common, if not generally approved. He had a larger-than-life personality and tended to dominate the gatherings we attended.

He became involved with one of my girlfriends, Stella. I do not know if she was part of his research, but sex and drugs were certainly prominent in their relationship. She later made a religious conversion, had an affair with her married religious teacher and then became pregnant by him. He made her have an abortion as he was not prepared to recognise the child as his. Tragically, Stella later ended her own life.

I was never interested in drugs and would not have accepted them if they had been offered. I had been wise enough to refuse the drug thalidomide which my doctor had recommended to me when I was pregnant with my second child Darrell. He was consequently born a normal healthy boy. However, there was one occasion when I was working at Pinewood, when one of the actors suggested I should try marijuana. I did accept then because

I knew him and trusted he would not give me something that would be risky or harmful. The substance I sampled when I arrived back home was contained in soft-centred chocolates – which I loved without any additional ingredients anyway! George and I were completely naïve about the use of drugs and we treated it as an experiment. He kept me under close watch to make sure I was safe and would not do anything silly. Typically, I think he even had a notepad to write down his observations – but no white coat! The effect was enjoyable and I had a pleasant high. The high lasted for a couple of days, but I still managed to continue with my professional work at Pinewood, although my behaviour toward people was noticeably different. But one psychedelic experience was enough. It was interesting and pleasurable, but I had no need to take drugs to make me relax or achieve a higher level of consciousness.

George had a full-time engineering job but kept having to take time off to deal with our legal matters. I had a series of jobs between film work. During the frenzied build up to the 1966 World Cup I tried to make some extra money by selling World Cup Willies. This was a small lion-based mascot which could be pinned onto clothing. It was no fun hawking these around newsagents and shops in the Wembley area where I lived before I left my husband. I later got a job as a confectionery buyer for Empire Stores based in Leicester Square. That was fun as I had to decide which chocolates to put in our shops and the sales people tried to persuade me to choose their wares. I received lots of chocolate during this time – a definite perk of the job!

One day Douglas Fairbanks Jr. introduced me to a Swedish judge, Gösta Wilkins, who had come to the UK to decide whether the new form of transport, the hovercraft designed by Sir Christopher Cockerell, was a ship or an aircraft. The first mention in the historical record of the principles behind hovering and hoverboats was by Swedish scientist Emanuel Swedenborg in 1716 and in 1915 the Austrian Dagobert Müller built the world's first air-cushion vehicle. Doug and Gösta invited me to join them for a trip on one of the first British prototypes based at Dover. It was exhilarating for me, as I have always loved fast movement on the water and this was certainly high-speed travel! It was an excellent day out and I enjoyed every moment. It was later determined that, legally, a hovercraft would be regarded as a ship.

I was working on various films during the '60s. The Harry Palmer films were made by EON Productions and *Funeral in Berlin* was being shot in Berlin. The leading lady playing the part of a German spy had to leave the cast and the producers and director were looking for a replacement. One of the German actors suggested his girlfriend, Eva Renzi, and she got the part. When they came back from the shoot, the director Guy Hamilton, was no longer on speaking terms with Eva. I don't know what happened in Berlin, but Guy used me as a go-between whenever he had something to communicate to Eva. She was furious and the atmosphere was not pleasant. I was asked to coach her and I felt let down that Guy and the producers had not asked me to play the lead. After all, I was born in Berlin, spoke German with a Berlin accent and my English didn't need any coaching! I think they were sorry they hadn't thought of it. At the end of the film, I actually did revoice Eva. Michael Caine (the male lead), with whom I got on well, told me as far as he was concerned that film was the first and last Eva Renzi would ever make in the UK. He was right.

This was the second time I missed out on having the leading part in an EON Production film. First, Daniela in *From Russia With Love*, and now I had lost out again!

* * * *

One day in 1968 when I was out shopping in Maida Vale, it started to rain heavily and so I found shelter in a nearby estate agents – Chesterton's. I was wet and bedraggled, but pretended I was looking to purchase a house. I perused the various properties for sale and saw an information sheet advertising 'A Leasehold Investment Property' for sale. It comprised of eleven flatlets, eight in occupation. It was in Broadhurst Gardens, West Hampstead. The asking price was only £10,000, but the lease was for a measly 23 years (expiring in 1991). It was an attractive price, but there was a catch – indeed, several. The property had tenants and one was 'protected'. However, we were aware of one extremely significant fact.

A recently enacted piece of legislation, the Leasehold Reform Act 1967, gave homeowners the right to purchase the freehold of a property subject to conditions. These were that the property be occupied solely as their residence for a minimum of five years, and the lease should have a minimum of 21 years to run. We saw it as an opportunity and took a calculated gamble. We decided to go ahead.

There was just one small problem – we had no money! My father spoke to a friend of his, Mr Instone Bloomfield, who owned a bank in Berkeley Square. He kindly arranged for us to have a loan on the property from the Heritable and General Investment Bank.

Once negotiations to purchase began, other complications arose. The sale was what is known as an 'executor's sale'. The deceased owner (Miss Allbutt) had obtained a licence from the freeholders way back in 1936 to use the premises as 'a first-class boarding house'. The tenancies were all originally 'oral tenancies'. The freeholders took a dim view when they learnt of the changes to separately let rooms and claimed an 'alleged breach' of covenant of the lease. This had to be resolved so that the tenants could be legalised before we purchased the house.

Buying the house was becoming exceedingly complicated and counsel's opinion was sought. Our solicitors (Neilson & Co.) regarded the opinion as bad news. They got cold feet and advised us to withdraw from the purchase.

But we had a simple solution to the problems; we would tell all the tenants that we would not be taking any rent and they would be guests in our home! On hearing this, our solicitor changed his mind and wrote to us saying, 'Your proposal appears to be ingenious, and the new price would certainly appear to justify the small risk now remaining'. The purchase price had now come down to a bargain £6,500. This was a reflection of the fact that, by taking possession, we would lose all possible income and were likely to incur further legal costs in doing so.

We finally completed in November 1968 and became the owners of a large house in multiple occupation. We needed it to become a house in single occupation very quickly, so we approached the tenants and advised them we would not be taking any rent and told them they were all guests in our home. But, could they kindly move out – at their own convenience, but as quickly as possible please, which, without any significant difficulties, they did. By January 1969 they had all gone.

There was one protected tenant, Miss Morgan, living in the house. She was an old, reclusive spinster who had been a friend of Miss Allbutt. When the house was up for sale, she had feared being kicked out of her home where she had lived for many years. We told her she could stay in the house indefinitely, rent-free. She was mightily relieved, but sadly Miss Morgan died just before Christmas 1968. After her death, her surviving relatives (two male nephews) came over and went through all her possessions looking for any valuables. They discarded piles of letters, documents, newspaper, photographs, military badges, theatre programmes and other bric-a-brac which she had hoarded over the years. We went through the remaining piles of 'rubbish' which the nephews left behind and discovered a treasure trove of fascinating memorabilia from which we were able to piece together her family history.

Miss May Leoniede King-Morgan was the daughter of Mr George King-Morgan. He was a flamboyant Irish entrepreneur who hailed from Dublin but lived in Liverpool for a while, and was involved in various business ventures. At one time he was a well-known operatic singer and performed in theatres and variety halls. He also toured with the original 'Biograph' from the Palace, London, showing animated pictures of the first South Africa War and also managed/owned the St James Picturedrome (an early cinema). His main sporting connection was being the business manager for George Hackenshmidt, the great Russian wrestling champion, with whom he spent nine years touring the world.

Miss Morgan had also lived in Liverpool around the time of the First World War. She helped to care for wounded soldiers and raised funds for them through charitable concerts, moving to London in the 1930s.

Another tenant, Mrs Gertie Maishment, had been there for many years. She lived in the basement flat and was a sort of housekeeper. She was also worried about her future, so she was thankful when we said she could also stay on, rent-free.

All the risks we had taken had paid off. With all the complications resolved, all we had to do now was sit it out for five years and then purchase the freehold. We would then be the owners of a substantial, desirable residence in a sought-after location and worth quite a bit more than the price we had paid.

What to do with all the extra space we had now acquired? At the start we occupied two huge rooms with ceilings over 11 feet high on the ground floor. We ate and slept in the lounge facing the garden and the children slept in the bedroom facing the road. As the tenants left we spread out to the upper floors. There were three rooms on the first level and we made Kerry's bedroom into one of them. We established our bedroom next to Kerry's and Darrell was placed above us on the second floor. We moved Gertie the housekeeper upstairs and this released the basement for refurbishment.

The late-Victorian house contained many original and fascinating features. One such was a free-standing, cast-iron stove in the basement embossed with the name 'Romesse'. George knew through his engineering connections that the Science Museum was interested in acquiring pieces of antique heating equipment for its Industrial Archaeology department. Our offer to donate it to the nation was gratefully accepted and the museum sent a crew around to dismantle it and carry it away. In due course we received a letter of thanks from the assistant keeper and later a large, glossy photograph showing the refurbished stove in all its splendid original glory. It is catalogued under the museum inventory number 1969-0472.

Close to our house at the top of Broadhurst Gardens was the Decca Recording Studios. From them we learnt that lots of musicians needed rehearsal space, so we decided to convert the large basement area which opened onto the garden, into a rehearsal room. There was a separate side entrance and it had its own toilet facilities and so could be isolated from the rest of the house. George enthusiastically set about the task. He did a complete refurbishment of the area, making it soundproof, attractive and comfortable. He built a special drummer's plinth with a solid concrete base and we moved my mother's grand piano down there. Darrell helped George and learnt a lot of useful practical skills by watching him. When the project was finished we told Decca about the availability of rehearsal space and together with our own advertising, a mixture of clients came and used the room. This included solo artists and groups.

On one occasion the rock group Pink Floyd booked the room for several days. We were not prepared for the huge removal van which pulled up outside our house. A team of roadies proceeded to unload huge amplifiers and other bulky equipment which they carried down and stacked up in the room.

All good stuff, but the house rocked – I mean literally rocked. We felt vibrations all around the house and the neighbours complained. We did not want to risk the same fate as when the Walls of Jericho fell down, so in the end, we had to restrict the type of client we could accommodate. It was great fun while it lasted. Some time later, the area around West Hampstead was hit by flash flooding and our lovely rehearsal room disappeared under several feet of water. Our tears only added to the lake that the basement room had become. Eventually, the water receded and George made the necessary repairs.

We applied to purchase the freehold in January 1973, while the market was rising, but by the time we completed the purchase, in late 1974, for an additional £5,300, property prices had fallen again.

We had a splendid few years in Broadhurst Gardens. I spent a lot of time with the children. I took them shopping and to the cinema and theatre and generally, we enjoyed ourselves as much as we could. George joined us for outings as well, when he wasn't working. There were lovely moments living in the house. I enjoyed having the space for us and the children to play and move around in. We played all sorts of games with them, including indoor badminton (courtesy of the 11 feet high ceilings) and we loved having so much room after the cramped flat in Maida Vale. I was able to forget our troubles when playing with the children and taking them out. We went on holidays with them to Devon and Cornwall in our little Mini.

Our garden in Broadhurst Gardens backed on to a large communal green space, more like a field, where on Guy Fawkes Night, the neighbours came and celebrated. George and the children made the guy which sat on top of a huge bonfire. Mike Flynn and his family next door had us all over to their house for refreshments after the ritual burning of the guy. We had other friendly neighbours – Maureen and Wolfgang Lass. They lived a couple of doors down from us. Their house also backed on to the field and it was a great environment for all the children to play in, which they did for many years. When they moved to Scotland, although we obviously couldn't see them as much as we had before, we did travel up and stay with them several times. Wolfgang ran the catering department at Culzean Castle on the Ayrshire coast. Part of the eighteenth-century country house was given to (the then) General Eisenhower as a holiday home. The magnificent clifftop position has commanding views overlooking the Firth of Clyde towards the Isle of Arran. The castle has movie connections too as it was used for some scenes in the 1973 cult film *The Wicker Man*.

The West Hampstead/Finchley Road district was a favoured area for people in the arts. One local resident with whom I became friends was Bernard Kops, the author and poet. Given that he was of Dutch-Jewish extraction we had a lot to discuss when he dropped in for tea. Another local resident I would sometimes meet when he walked his dog was John Justin, famed for his role in the 1940 film *The Thief of Bagdad*.

By 1972 Rabbi Dow Marmur was the minister at Alyth. He and his wife, Fredzia and their children, Viveca, Michael and Lisa became good friends of my family. I fondly remember their house in Golders Green where we often enjoyed informal visits as well as the beautiful Passover Seder (supper) evening, which Dow led.

During this time, the children were working towards their bar and bat mitzvahs, the Jewish coming of age for 13-year-old boys and (as far as my father was concerned), 16 years for girls. In 1974 Darrell would be thirteen and Kerry would be sixteen, so we could have both ceremonies on the same day. Dad and I worked with the children on their Torah portions. I must explain for the non-Jewish reader that the girls and boys read a portion of the Torah, (the Five Books of Moses) during the service in Hebrew with the English translation. This is followed by the Reading of the Law in English called the Haftorah, all delivered from the pulpit. This is how it is done in the Reform Movement and the event is extremely significant in the Jewish faith.

The fact that the recently retired senior rabbi of the Reform Movement was going to conduct the bar and bat mitzvah service for his grandchildren made it doubly appealing to the congregation. The day dawned and the children and I went to Alyth for the service. The synagogue was overflowing with congregants and I along with Mum and the children were sitting in the front row. Dad, in his gown, was on the bimah - the raised dais with the lectern standing on it. The children both read their portions beautifully and we were all very proud of them. We then went on to the West London Synagogue for a celebration luncheon. In the evening Kerry and Darrell had a party with their friends at Alyth. It was a day to remember.

All this was going on while George and I were in the middle of our case in the High Court, as well as buying the freehold of our house in Broadhurst Gardens. I had already started studying for my A levels as well as working on films and commercials for TV. Our lives were indeed a kaleidoscope of contrasting activities.

A united family - Mum, Dad, me, George, Kerry and Darrell

Joint Bat and Bar-mitzvah, 1974

113

Sketch of Darrell by George

CHAPTER 12

RETURN TO BERLIN

My parents had retired to Mallorca in 1968 after Dad's retirement. They had been to Mallorca many times on holiday and enjoyed the weather there. Mum always wanted to be in the sun, so they found a flat in what was then a little fishing village called El Arenal, not far from the capital Palma. The apartment overlooked the sea and they spent many happy years there. It was always a dilemma for rabbis to know what to do after they retired. If they continued attending the synagogue services, then the succeeding rabbi might feel uncomfortable. On the other hand, if they left to go to another synagogue, it would look as though they were abandoning and being disloyal to their former congregation. To go to another country to retire was ideal, because then they could come back to the synagogue as honoured guests.

Dad became involved with the embryonic Jewish congregation in Palma and it flourished under his guidance. A senior Catholic bishop came to one of the services and that was a milestone for the congregation. Dad found many of his former friends came on holiday there and attended his services. Dad had been instrumental in forming a new congregation in Cardiff in Wales and the friends he made then, such as Michael and Lillian Bogod, became closer to Dad and Mum in Mallorca where they had and still have a holiday home. They and their family hosted me and Kerry as well when we went to visit. They were invaluable friends as Mum got older and I still see them when they come to London.

Going back to my marriage with George, although my father never discussed his feelings about it to me, he could see how happy I was with him. He also knew George was not objecting to the children being brought up in the Jewish tradition. This was good of George, but it meant he would be deprived of the Christmas tree that was in his home when he was growing up. He felt it would be inappropriate and confuse the children, so he made that concession for our family, one of many. Maybe my parents realised something of this as we gradually built up a good relationship with Mum, and Dad eventually reconciled himself to the situation as well. In fact, relations improved so much that when they visited London, they sometimes stayed with us at our home in Broadhurst Gardens.

They were most impressed with the property and its location in North London. George's Mum came as well and both she and my parents met there. During one visit, we had a shock when Dad had a heart attack and was taken to the New End hospital in Hampstead. To our great relief he recovered and then Mum and Dad returned to their home in Mallorca. In retrospect, it was better that he became ill in London rather than Mallorca because I believe he received better treatment here.

As the reader is probably already aware, so many different things were happening at the same time, that it is not possible to relate them in chronological order. While all the above was taking place, I was working on feature films, a TV series and the odd commercial and trying to get into television as a presenter. I met Michael Barratt at Lime Grove and he tried to help me, but I never did get to present on his TV show *Nationwide*. It wasn't until later that the BBC allowed a woman to co-present such a programme. I did manage to get an interview with ATV, the regional company based in Birmingham, for a woman's afternoon chat programme. George put up an aerial on a high mast and we were able to receive a grainy picture of the test transmission. This was occurring while my ex-husband was still persisting with the legal applications to try to wrest the care and control of my children away from us.

About this time, I revoiced Michelle Mercier in a film first called *Dubious Patriot*, starring Tony Curtis, but released as *You Can't Win Them All*. It was directed by Peter Collinson who was a good friend of mine for many years.

I had always admired Roger Moore as an actor. He was tremendously good looking and was a matinee idol of mine. In 1962, I was working in Pinewood Studios on the first Bond film, *Dr. No*, when I was also asked to revoice a young actress on *The Saint* series which came out the same year. Suddenly, I was meeting the star of the series, Roger Moore, face to face. He was as charming a man in real life as the character he played in the episodes of *The Saint* and we got on well together. I revoiced many of the young women who appeared in the series and through that Roger and I became firm friends.

We renewed our friendship when he was filming *The Persuaders* with Tony Curtis. I was asked to revoice various female characters as I had done on *The Saint*. This was a real treat as, often, when the work on one film or series ends, you may never see the actors again. Now I was working with Roger once more and met his co-star, Tony Curtis as well. When I was told I would be working with Tony Curtis in the sound studio, I was informed that he was a demanding person and difficult to get on with. That made me nervous and I entered the studio with trepidation.

I started my revoicing first and then Tony worked on replacing parts of his own voice. Often, when filming outside, there can be noises from traffic or planes, which makes it difficult to hear the actor's voice. That's when he or she needs to revoice their own words in the sound studio so they can be clearly heard. This is what Tony was doing. At the end of the session, we talked and he took me out for lunch. Over the meal we got on well and he was natural and easy to talk to. I felt so relaxed with him that I told him how I had been warned against him. He laughed and said he was only 'difficult' if someone was not doing their job properly, but with someone like me who was a professional and good at their work, he was fine. As we were both Jewish, I told him a little about my family background, which he found interesting. He invited me to his end-of-series party for *The Persuaders* in July 1971 which was a great occasion. Roger and Tony had not got on too well during the series so both had their own end-of-series party, but I think I was the only person to be invited to both!

During the filming of *The Persuaders*, I told Roger Moore how much my children liked the show and especially him. He surprised and pleased me by saying he would come round to the house and say hello to them. So one evening a limo drew up outside our house and, lo and behold, Roger Moore stepped out! Opposite us there lived some young girl tenants and they must have seen Roger arriving. They were leaning out of the window, staring and then the whole of that part of the street followed suit, gawping and looking through their windows to see where he was going. Well, the children were overwhelmed and so thrilled to meet Roger. He was so sweet with them and made their day and mine.

I often had lunch with Roger and Michael Caine and they introduced me to other well-known actors such as Robert Wagner and Maurice Denham. On one occasion I took Kerry and Darrell with me to Pinewood and showed them the sets and introduced them to Sydney Tafler. He was one of the villains in *The Spy Who Loved Me* and was cast as the captain of the gigantic super tanker The Liparus. They thoroughly enjoyed their outing.

* * * *

In 1971 I narrated a documentary called *Night Flight To Berlin* and this had made me think about my birthplace. My father had been invited to speak at a conference in Berlin in September that year, so George and I decided to visit Berlin to coincide with my parents being there.

This was the first time of going back to my roots since I had left as a child of almost four years of age in 1939. I was a little apprehensive as to what I would find. My expectations were of a bleak landscape.

After World War Two ended, Berlin had become isolated behind the Iron Curtain. When the East German government, under the command of the Soviet Union, later built the Berlin Wall, it sealed off the city almost completely from the West. The Cold War years were full of international tensions. Berlin was constantly in the news and many thought a third world war was inevitable. I was curious about my home town and wanted to see where I had been born and where my mother had grown up. I wanted to see where my mother's parents' house stood and find the flat that Mum and Dad had lived in.

I knew that I was born in what later became the communist Eastern Zone, but I did not know if any of the old buildings were still standing.

George and I took the car ferry from Harwich to the Hook of Holland. We watched with some trepidation as our Austin Mini was hoisted onto the ship and lowered into a hold. Not as now, when you simply drive the car on board. We then made our way down to our cabin for the night crossing. The next morning we left the boat at 7.00 am and had breakfast at a little place called Hallingen. We drove through Hanover and after stopping overnight at Braunschweig, we continued to the East German border. There was a lengthy delay at the customs control while our papers and our car were inspected. The journey from the border to West Berlin was easy driving on the almost empty autobahn. There were more custom controls at the entry to West Berlin. I thought we would never get there.

The first thing we did when we arrived in Berlin was to see my parents at the Savoy Hotel where they were staying. The next day we went with them to see the Brandenburg Gate, the Victory Statue and other tourist places of interest. This was my first taste of my hometown and I was fascinated. We had lunch and then visited the large synagogue in the Oranienburger Strasse where Dad had given the last service before he was arrested by the Nazis. We managed to spend some happy hours together, but Dad did not have much time as his main concern was to address the conference the next day. After that they returned to the UK, but we stayed on a few days longer.

The apartment in which we had lived was now in East Berlin and we thought getting there might not be easy. We went to the East/West border crossing at Checkpoint Charlie and showed the guards our passports and then we were allowed through. We made our way to Pieskower Weg and found the apartment house where Mum and Dad had lived and where I had been born. There we met a lady, Madam Pliquet, who had lived next door to my parents in Berlin in the 1930s and she had been friendly with them. She was still living there with her husband and invited us to come up to the apartment. She hated the Nazis and now she hated the Communists and told us she refused to hang out the Nazi flag and now was again refusing to hang out the Soviet flag. We were so impressed with her courage and decided we would take her some treats of things that she hadn't seen in years.

We then went to look at other places of interest, and had a proper look at the wall the Russians had built to divide Berlin. It was all depressingly sad and East Berlin was such a bleak place to be living in. We went into a restaurant near my birthplace, to try the local cuisine, but there was hardly anything on the menu except for speck (pig fat). Apart from being unsuitable for a Jewish girl, it was quite disgusting and so George and I didn't eat. Queues formed in the street when a stall was put up with a few loaves of bread! It was a pitiful sight and we were pleased to get back to the West. However, a few days later we again waited to cross the border at Checkpoint Charlie, as we were taking our food basket to Madam Pliquet. This time the border control asked us if we had anything to declare and we were really scared he might find the food we had brought over. To our relief the guard didn't find anything, but he did espy a few tourist postcards of West Berlin. He was very interested in them and examined them thoroughly. I'm sure he would have much rather been in the West than doing his job in East Berlin. What he failed to find was that our basket for Madam Pliquet contained real coffee, chocolates, butter, eggs, rolls etc. She cried with joy, saying she hadn't tasted these things since before the Russian occupation.

At the end of the visit to Berlin, I was pleased to have seen where I came from, but the huge contrast between East and West Berlin was dreadful to have experienced. The people who lived in the East were the same as the Berliners who had lived in the West of the city. They were used to a certain standard of life and now they lived in poverty. Families had been split apart, and life in the East became one of hardship. Nobody dared say anything critical of the regime in public places, as we were told there were secret devices to detect any unrest. Dire punishment awaited those who did complain.

I was relieved when our visit ended and we were back in good old Broadhurst Gardens.

It took us three years to obtain the freehold of the house, during which time the property boom rose and fell. Then in 1974, having purchased the freehold, we were in a position to sell the house. We did so, but for a much lesser price than if we had been able to sell it at the height of the market. However, after purchasing a smaller house in Hendon, we did have a bit of extra money.

We had always thought that a motor van would enable us to explore not just the countryside of England, but also further afield. To that end we bought a Leyland Sherpa van and George completely remodelled it so that we could sleep in it. He installed a raising roof, and fitted-out the interior to include a fold-down bed, a kitchen area and a chemical toilet. It was a real home and looked elegant. I made the curtains and cushions and we used the van on a regular basis. We originally had big plans to go round the world with the children and take them out of school for a year to show them the wonders of other countries. One of the reasons that stopped us in the end was the price of fuel. We reckoned that a gallon of petrol would soon cost us £1 and that was too much.

When Darrell began attending William Ellis School, which was then a voluntary aided grammar school, we became heavily involved with the Parents' Association. The school was one of those being proposed by the Inner London Education Authority for conversion to a comprehensive by amalgamating with the local girls schools. We were strongly opposed to William Ellis losing its status as a grammar school as we favoured selection. There was a great deal of discussion amongst parents, but the members of the existing PA supported the change. The 1973 year intake was an active one and managed to vote out the existing PA officers. This caused a mini-crisis and the old guard walked out and set up a rival association called the Friends of William Ellis. The headmaster, Mr Sydney Baxter, spent more time than was prudent trying to placate both camps and admitted he was neglecting educational matters.

We became good friends with Margaret and Brian Alzano, the parents of Darrell's school friend Julian. Brian was elected as chairman of the PA and under his leadership it organised many successful fund-raising events. Money had been raised in previous years, but these events were much more splendid and stylish than before. The summer fete and donkey derby in

1974 alone raised over £2,500. The fete was opened by Fenella Fielding, a friend of Beatrice Vine, a parent who had two sons at the school.

The PA needed a newsletter and George was voted editor and volunteered to produce it. Brian, Margaret, Beatrice and George and I formed the editorial committee and held many discussions long into the night about its policy and content. The previous PA had produced the usual dull, single sheet of typed notes, but George had grander ideas. This was long before computers and desktop publishing were available, but he designed and produced a large format, multi-page publication with bold headlines, photographs, interviews, adverts, a letters column and cartoons. It was called the WESPA Whisper and had an immediate impact. After the first issue the entire 30-strong teaching staff sent a letter of protest condemning the printing of one particular letter. But unbeknown to them the headmaster, Mr Baxter, had sent a letter of congratulations and both letters were printed side by side in the next issue creating even more furore.

Through our involvement with the PA, I got to see a lot of the headmaster. When I met him in his office to discuss various school matters he made it clear that he would like to become friendlier with me than a normal headmaster/ parent relationship would imply. On the occasion of the PA's President Ball Dinner and Dance, he made up some pretext to speak to me privately in his office. I admit I must have looked fetching in my ballgown and it took some effort for me to quell his male ardour. I reminded him that his dear wife was in the school hall serving her favourite culinary contribution: 'Devils on Horseback'.

In the event we lost the fight to keep William Ellis as a grammar school and after Darrell left to go up to Liverpool University, the school became a comprehensive. But we had done our best.

CHAPTER 13
LAW STUDENT

By the time the court proceedings finally ended in 1975 the UK was experiencing the three-day week, during Edward Heath's government. I felt I had done a good job of pleading my case in front of the president of the Family Division and I was conscious of the many women in my position who were unable to put their cases effectively. For example, in our case, our solicitors would brief a barrister and we would have a conference with him, only to find that on the day of the hearing, he would have another case to go to and we would find ourselves with a different barrister who had no knowledge of the previous hearings. There was no continuity. This meant we sat there and listened to all sorts of inaccuracies which we couldn't correct. How frustrating is that? Also, not everyone has the confidence to act for themselves and so they have to rely on lawyers. As we saw, they were not always reliable.

But now the situation had changed and I decided to become a barrister. I would study law so that I could help people in my situation, knowing what it was like to be terrified of going to court and possibly losing one's children in divorce cases.

I was almost 40 years old and had never even thought about any other profession besides acting. After all I had started acting when I was a young child, yet here I was, embarking on the path to becoming a professional lawyer. Having left school before doing my A-Level exams, I had to return to college to study for the missing qualifications. I managed to do this in one academic year in 1974. The subjects I chose were Economics and British Government. Mr Philip Shaffer taught me Economics at Kilburn Polytechnic and he was a great teacher. I met him and his delightful wife socially when they lived in Kingsbury and they invited me over for tea. I was still working in the sound studios at the same time as taking the courses, but I did well in the final exams.

I was accepted at Middlesex Polytechnic to do my Council for Academic Awards, (CNAA) degree. It was the equivalent of the LLB Law degree. I had not done too well academically at Maida Vale High School and so lacked confidence in my ability to start a law degree course, but I had made my mind up and would jolly well do my best. It was a good thing I had spent a year studying for my A-Levels, as that brought me back to the discipline of writing essays and notes of the lectures on the various Law subjects. I found some of the work hard, but because I was determined to succeed as a lawyer, I ploughed on. I did enjoy the intellectual legal arguments and at the end of the three years, I felt at home at the Poly. Of course, this was also where George and I had met ten years earlier at the guitar classes, so that was quite a squaring of the circle. We had good tutors and I became friendly with one of them, a New Zealander called Ian McDuff, who was living here with his partner. George and I met them socially and particularly remember a smashing New Year's Eve party at the end of 1975.

In July 1977 the degree exam results came out. Everyone was pushing and shoving to see the grades on the board. I finally got there, saw my name and realised that I had passed. This was so exciting and I felt the three years' hard work had now truly paid off.

English barristers are still required to join one of the four Inns (Gray's Inn, Middle Temple Inn, Lower Temple Inn and Lincoln's Inn) to qualify as a barrister. I favoured Middle Temple and so the next step was to enrol there and study at the Inns of Court School of Law for the Bar Finals.

Another requirement to becoming a barrister is to eat a prescribed number of dinners in Middle Temple Hall during term time. Dinners in Hall meant dining with other students and barristers and were formal events. The first Dining Term was to start four days after my degree results had come out.

We were allowed to bring guests in from time to time. I invited George, of course, but occasionally I also took along other guests. One was my old friend Jerome Karet. He was then a solicitor and because of the assumed superiority of barristers over solicitors, felt slightly uncomfortable being in the inner sanctum of Middle Temple Hall.

The hall at Middle Temple is one of the finest examples of an Elizabethan hall in the country and was built between 1562 and 1573. It has an impressive double hammer beam roof carved out of oak trees from Windsor Forest. Shakespeare's play *Twelfth Night* had its first performance there in 1602 and it is believed that he was included in the cast. The long hall has a dais at the far end where the Bencher Judges sit at an imposing high table, eating their dinners. We lesser mortals who are the pupil barristers sitting with our sponsor barristers and other barristers, sit below the platform at right angles to the top table, in rows of benches and the atmosphere is medieval.

The one-year course at the law school includes practical exercises. After passing the final exam, you will be 'called to the Bar'. You then need to complete a one-year pupillage as a pupil barrister and part of this pupillage is usually unpaid.

I started the term at the School of Law on 9th January 1978. The course was quite difficult and I took Family Law, Criminal Procedure, EEC Law, Revenue Law (which I found the most difficult) and Evidence. We did a practical course as well, which involved going to different courts, such as a Crown, Criminal, Magistrates and the High Court. We had one-to-one tutorials and during this time I also helped to arrange 'moots'. These consisted of pupils taking on the prosecuting and defence barristers' roles in usually fictitious cases which were then judged by our tutors.

At one of the cases I was attending as a pupil in the High Court, I saw David Mellor, the barrister and later MP, conducting a case brilliantly. I approached him and introduced myself and when he heard I was studying for the Bar, he invited me to his home. I met his then wife Judith, and they helped me a lot. He was trying to become a Member of Parliament for the Conservatives at that time and after I passed the Bar exams, I assisted him with his campaign. Subsequently, he invited me to be his political research assistant in the House of Commons, but I will come back to that later.

As pupils we had to have sponsors who were already practising barristers and mine was Nigel Sweeney. We got on well and I told him all about my experiences in the High Court and the appearances in front of Sir George Baker. I ate my dinners with Nigel and on these occasions we met the Judges of Middle Temple. Each Inn has their own judges who sit at the High Table, but sometimes they mingled with the pupils.

One evening, sitting at the long table in Middle Temple, Nigel pointed out that Sir George Baker, with whom I had crossed swords during the long drawn out court proceedings, was coming our way. He stopped opposite me and sat down facing me across the table. Next to him was seated Judge Alan King-Hamilton. He was a member of my father's congregation and we, that is Mum, Dad, me and the children, spent time with them on holidays together with his daughter Jane and her family. The president saw me talking to him and asked how we knew each other. I told him I had known the King-

Hamiltons for years. (Would this have helped me, had Sir George known about it when I appeared before him?) He addressed each pupil around the table asking them what had motivated them to take up Law. The president obviously did not recognise me, but my sponsor, Nigel, who was a friend of both the judges, was taking an impish delight in the situation. The president spoke to some of the other new faces sitting at the table and asked them how long they had studied and whether they had any family who were lawyers.

The president then turned to me once more and asked me the same questions. I said that personal experiences had convinced me for the need to go into Family Law. At this point, Nigel could not contain himself any longer. He introduced me as Nikki van der Zyl and told Sir George that he himself already knew me well. He told Sir George that my children and I had been in a case in front of him for four years. Sir George, who had the air of a benign uncle up to that moment, went white. "What is your name again?" he asked, because he had not recognised the name 'van der Zyl'.

Nigel then explained that I had been known to him as 'Mrs. Rooker'.

"Not that case!" he exclaimed. Judge King-Hamilton was concerned at Sir George's change of demeanour and asked what the trouble was. Sir George said he well remembered having me in front of him for years and had never expected to see me again. After that, we started to talk and remarkably, we got on well. He said it was his birthday that day (25th April) and I told him that it was my birthday on the 27th. We both laughed and any tension that had existed began to ease. He asked after the children and it was agreed we would see each other again at the next dinner.

We received our results from the School of Law on 12th July 1978. I was relieved to have passed and I was called to the Bar two weeks later at a special dinner in Middle Temple Hall. In the official jargon of the ancient ceremony, I was 'Called to the Degree of the Utter Bar'. Once again, all my hard work had paid off.

It was a fantastic evening and my class and I celebrated in our new wigs and gowns. George came and took photos of me and my friends and with the judges. Afterwards, we all went on to the Waldorf Hotel and continued celebrating there. We didn't get home that night till the early hours.

I don't remember exactly when it was that I felt that Middle Temple Hall could do with livening up. It was normally a sombre place. I suppose the tall ceilings and its long benches and tables with the judges looking down at us green pupils sitting there, rather like the scene from the film *Oliver Twist*, didn't lend itself to having much fun. At the time of the dinners I became friendly with Judge Anthony Babington and I have happy memories of him when we shared jokes and thoughts together while we dined.

Sometime after the call to the Bar in 1978 I suggested to him that we should have a dinner dance in the Hall. He was quite taken aback and said there had never been any such event in the Hall before, to which I replied that it was high time, therefore, that something should take place now. A twinkle appeared in his eye and he eventually agreed. I don't know with whom he discussed this, but a few weeks later the dinner dance certainly did take place. Judges danced with pupil barristers and pupil barristers danced with their sponsors and people who didn't normally get a chance to talk together, socialised and the whole evening was very merry and a great success. Many years later, Anthony Arlidge, known to all as AA, built on this and introduced the first concert in 1991. As Master of Entertainments, he continued with serious and light-hearted music, play readings, and theatre performances. Well-known actors have appeared giving readings as well. Dancing is now a regular feature.

Marshalling is a valuable part of a pupil lawyer's training. Being a marshal does not mean wearing a shiny badge and carrying a pistol! Marshalling involves sitting next to the judge in court and following the proceedings. It can last for one day or a week. Marshalling gives the pupil barrister the opportunity to find out in practice, rather than via the theory taught during the Bar Finals, of how the judge comes to his or her decision. It lets them observe the rules of procedure and evidence in action and the 'do's and don'ts' of advocacy.

Judge Babington had asked me to marshal with him in his court, the Knightsbridge Crown Court, a week before the results had come out. After retiring to chambers we discussed the case and I contributed my thoughts. Pupil barristers usually approach a judge to ask if they may marshal for them, so it was a great honour to be asked.

I was thrilled when both he and Sir George wanted me to marshal for them, one in the Crown Court and the other in the Family Court that I knew so well!

Judge Babington not only treated me to lunch at Knightsbridge Crown Court, but took me and my husband George out regularly for drinks. It is usual to marshal for about a week, but my marshalling with him, on that occasion, went on for two weeks. On the last day he discharged the jury and started another case. At lunch I met Judge Kessel who told me to call him Harold. I was already calling Babington, Babs and Sir George, George and I felt privileged to be on first name terms with these judges. We'd become so friendly with Anthony Babington that he used to come over to our house for dinner with George and me and met some of our friends.

Babington was also a committee member of the Garrick Club, an enthusiastic member of the writers' organisation Pen and the author of a number of highly regarded books. Babington died in 2004. Tim Heald said in the obituary he wrote, 'He was also a good companion, a bon viveur, a flirtatious old gent, and kind and gentle to a fault'. I certainly second that!

CHAPTER 14
THE QUEEN AND I

It was a custom that pupils coming to the end of their law studies were invited to spend the Easter weekend at Cumberland Lodge in Windsor Great Park. In 1977 it was the turn of my class to attend. Jean Austin, the administrator of Middle Temple arranged this and it was an occasion for pupils, tutors and judges to come together on an informal basis. We studied during the day and on the Saturday evening, Miss Austin came round to some of us to say we were invited to go to St George's Chapel for the Easter service next day. A chosen few were also to meet the Queen Mother at Royal Lodge after the service.

When I was asked, I thought it was a joke. She said, "It's no joke," and explained that the Queen Mother usually came to Cumberland Lodge to listen to the 'moots', on a Saturday afternoon. These were like little plays, as I explained earlier, and the Queen Mother used to enjoy them, but this time we were invited to come socially to the house as it was Easter. Judge Alan King-Hamilton had been invited to the service but not to the reception afterwards. He asked me if I could get him an invite, but it was not in my hands. I couldn't understand why I had been invited, so asked Jean to explain. She said that the idea was to let those pupils from abroad, who might never have the chance to see the Queen Mother again, meet her tomorrow. I said I was not one of those, so she said that because they might be nervous and I was so good at putting people at ease, she thought I would be a good person to be there to smooth their path. I thought that was a nice compliment.

Sunday morning dawned and I, the daughter of a prominent rabbi was going to church! The entire Royal Family were sitting in their allotted places in the church and the chaplain gave the sermon, which just so happened to be about the Jewish Passover. He said, amongst other things, that the Jews roast a whole lamb for the Passover supper. This was news to me! Anyway, after the service we all went to Royal Lodge to meet the Queen Mother. We were greeted at the front door by a member of the staff and shown into a large room overlooking the gardens. It was airy and light. The Queen Mum had lined up the whole family for us to meet. There was Her Majesty the Queen, Princess Margaret, Princes Charles, Andrew and Edward and Prince Philip.

In 1953, when I was 18, my parents bought a television set in order to watch Queen Elizabeth II's coronation service. The BBC had been transmitting programmes before the war, but only a few had the money to buy TV sets. Now, with the immense interest in the Royal Family, sales of TVs expanded. I relished the time we were able to watch the programmes.

Also in that same year, Dad had been invited to the Guildhall, to hear Prince Philip speak, but he and Mum were going on holiday, so Dad gave me his tickets. I had never been to the Guildhall before and it was breathtakingly beautiful. I went with Robert Rietti and we sat at a table facing the top table, but also opposite Prince Philip. During the meal, his eye caught mine and he smiled at me. I was the youngest person there by about 30 years and the Prince was sitting between two important, elderly people. He gestured to me to accompany him out of the room. I laughed and shook my head. After all, I was with my friend and I loved Prince Philip's wife, so I did not fancy any hanky-panky with him.

Now, I was in Royal Lodge and this was the first time I was seeing him, 20-odd years later, since that occasion. He looked very handsome still and it was good to see him again.

I had practised my curtsies and as I moved down the line of the Royals, the Queen Mum introduced the Queen to us by saying, "I would like you to meet my daughter."

I have always admired the Queen, from the early days when she was Princess Elizabeth. I liked her friendliness and her dignity and when her father died and she became Queen, she visited all the London suburbs. I was still a schoolgirl, but I found out where she was going to be and got there after school in time to see her drive past. I collected photos of her and generally thought she was marvellous.

I have to say the Queen still looked lovely. She is vivacious and has a marvellous complexion. She is interested in everything and is very knowledgeable. She is gracious, intelligent, charismatic and has a good sense of humour. The Queen Mother also shared this quality.

After having gone down the Royal line and performing all my curtsies, we broke up into little groups. I found myself in the group with the chaplain's wife. As in synagogue, I was always at my mother's (the rabbi's wife's) side after the service, so now I was at the chaplain's wife's side. How fitting! She was quite charming and asked me how I liked her husband's sermon. I hesitated because Jean Austin had told me not to say anything about my being Jewish, but in the end I did say that Dad was a well-known rabbi and I had never heard of Jewish people nowadays roasting a whole lamb! I politely said one or two other things, but praised her husband for the interesting sermon. The chaplain's wife pointed across the room and said, "Do go and tell the chaplain what you have told me, he'll be fascinated and say I asked you to go and see him."

I could see him at the other end of the room. He was a tall man with a slight stoop and he was chatting with the Queen. I gingerly weaved my way through all the Royal groupings and finally reached him. He was charming and politely asked me if I would like a drink. I don't drink, so asked for an orange juice, which he gave me. I told him about Dad and the things in his sermon that I had spoken of with his wife. He was not madly interested in me and wanted to get back to speaking to the Queen. I couldn't blame him as she was much more interesting than me. I was making my way back to the chaplain's wife, when he called after me. I turned round and he gestured to me. I put my finger on my chest and mouthed 'me?' He nodded for me to come back. I then retraced my steps round the groups and returned to him. He said, "The Queen would like me to present you." We were all wearing name tags and so he did present me officially and I once again curtsied to Her Majesty. We had been told to address her as Ma'am, so I said something like "pleased to meet you Ma'am."

She smiled and there was a distinct twinkle in her eye. I felt I had known her all my life. We talked about many things. While I had been speaking to the chaplain, the Queen, who was standing next to him, had been talking to someone else and I overheard her saying that the Chief Rabbi had been to Buckingham Palace and had not eaten there. Well, I opened the conversation by saying that I had heard her say this. I told her that if the reason for him not eating there was because it wasn't kosher, then he was obviously unaware that she had a kosher kitchen at Buck House. She smiled and agreed.

I said my father was a Reform rabbi at West London Synagogue, where he was the senior rabbi. She thought she had met him. We started talking about religion and I remarked that although the saying was 'money is the root of all evil', I felt it was actually religion that was the root of all evil, causing so many wars. True religion should just mean we are all good to each other. At that point, she put her hand on my arm and the official voice she usually used flew out of the window as she said, "Oh my dear, I do so agree with you." She was so easy to talk to.

She asked me what I thought about the recent talks between Israel's Prime Minister Begin and President Carter at Camp David in the US. I said I'd love to have been a fly on the wall and heard what they had to say. She replied, "So would I."

I then said, "What would they have made of us buzzing around them, the Queen of England and me?" She roared with laughter. I told her I used to wait for her to come by in her car when she was visiting all the boroughs of London, after she became Queen. I also said I was sure that if she wasn't who she was, we would be exchanging phone numbers and would meet for coffee next week. I could tell she agreed. Our birthdays fall in the same week and I told her that Taureans like us are the best.

We also spoke about education. Her Majesty said that Prince Edward, who at that moment was carrying the tray of drinks around, doesn't like doing maths, but has to do it. I pointed out that that was all very laudable, but that she could send Edward to whichever school she wanted. However, with limited funds, families like ours had to send the children to a state school in our area. These were not always the best schools. Then we talked about the different levels of education there are in England. We spoke for quite a long time and then she said she had to circulate but took me along with her.

She spoke to a group of young people from the Commonwealth and addressed a young man from Singapore. As we had just been speaking about education, she asked him about that. He was overwhelmed at speaking with the Queen of England and stuttered something about a girl genius who could add up any numbers inside her head, just like a robot! The Queen turned to me and I shrugged and said, "What else does she do?" The Queen repeated this in a sort of Jewish voice that I had used for fun and we both burst out laughing. After a little more banter, she really did have to meet some more of the Commonwealth pupil barristers.

I was then approached by Princess Margaret, who was smoking and had a lot of ash at the end of her cigarette. I passed her an ashtray and we started to talk. I was telling her about my work on the Bond films and she was getting interested, when unfortunately, the senior judge in charge of the visit, informed us it was time to leave and I had to excuse myself. On the way out there was a queue to say 'goodbye' to the Queen Mum, our lovely hostess, but when I reached her, she took me into the room adjoining the one we were in and asked, "Do you like dogs?" I assured her I did. She then proceeded to call the corgis. They came bounding up and we fed them. They had to jump up in the air to catch the biscuits. They were so appealing. The Queen Mother then said she had a favour to ask me. She explained that she loved coming to dinner at Middle Temple Hall, but was seldom invited to attend and could I arrange for her to be asked. I said I would do my best.

When I got back to Middle Temple, I went to see Jean Austin and told her what had been requested. Miss Austin then explained to me that the Queen Mother was the patron of Middle Temple and, as such, was the hostess. She didn't require an invitation to attend her own dinner party. I was sure the Queen Mother was not aware of this, so asked Miss Austin to convey this to her. I hope she did, but I never did get the chance to meet the Queen Mum again.

On the coach going back to Cumberland Lodge, everyone wanted to know what the Queen and I were giggling about. I told them how great she was and what we had talked about. This was one of the most memorable days of my life and I have never forgotten it. I even wrote a poem about it.

Coming full circle, in 2002 the Queen celebrated her Golden Jubilee and the London Borough of Barnet invited me to compose a special poem for inclusion in the souvenir programme. The brochure was to commemorate the Queen's visit to Barnet in June 2002, which comprised part of her Jubilee tour of the United Kingdom. Barnet hosted the visit on behalf of the North London boroughs.

CHAPTER 15
A PUPIL LAWYER

Simultaneous to being a full-time law student, I was still busy with my revoicing work in films and television series. Now that the law studies were completed I expected to begin work as a pupil barrister and spend the rest of my life in the legal profession. But, as so often happened in my life, an unforeseen opportunity would divert me from that course.

I had been studying European Economic Community (EEC) law as one of my subjects during the Bar Finals. Unbeknown to me, and I expect most people, the EEC provided internships (traineeships in EEC-speak) for graduates who wanted to become familiar with the workings of this burgeoning organisation. These interns were known as *stagiaires* and were mostly based in Brussels. The duration of the training was normally five months and a small living allowance was paid.

One of the tutors, Professor Fawcett, suggested I apply for an internship (called a *stage* in Brussels, pronounced 'starj') as I spoke German and had a good knowledge of French. He told me that it was necessary to apply the year before the *stage* started. The EEC offices are located in Brussels, Strasbourg and Luxembourg. George and I decided we would combine a holiday in Belgium with lodging a personal application for a *stage* in Brussels. We thought we had to go to Luxembourg to do this, so in September 1978 we drove there in our motor van, passing many historic places on the way. We arrived there, tired, in the evening.

The next morning, we made our way to the EEC offices and saw a Miss Floch. She explained that the person we needed to see was Herr Wolfgang Kraus, the administrator for the *stagiaires* in Brussels. We hadn't made sufficient enquiries before leaving home and we were in the wrong country. No matter, we were enjoying travelling and so we departed Luxembourg the next day and headed north-west towards Brussels, 150 miles away. It gave us the opportunity to spend a night near Waterloo and visit the site of the famous battlefield.

Next morning, we drove into Brussels and I had my first glimpse of the Berlaymont building. The Berlaymont is the iconic star-shaped office tower that houses the headquarters of the European Commission. We went for a long walk around Brussels and familiarised ourselves with the city. George and I do not drink but always like to find a cosy café for our daily coffee and cake. Brussels was no exception. I liked what I saw of the town and particularly the main square where we watched artists sketching portraits.

I met Herr Kraus and we had a good meeting. I told him my story about leaving Berlin, my reason for taking up law after the long battle in the High Court and my role in the Bond films. I think he was quite impressed. Although he wasn't supposed to take on students older than 32, he said it was no use being the head of the *stagiaires* if he couldn't make or break the rules every now and then. I would be 44 when I started the *stage* the following year, but he said he would make an exception for me. He agreed to accept me for the 1979 *stage*. I was thrilled as it would mean meeting people from other countries and getting to know how the EEC worked.

* * * *

Joe Jackson's chambers were one of the best Family Law chambers around and as I wanted to be a Family Law barrister, it made sense to try to secure a pupillage with them. A pupillage lasts six months and is essential for every budding barrister. I was lucky enough to be accepted there with Paul Focke. I started with Paul at no. 1 Mitre Court Buildings, Kings Bench Walk in October 1978. Margaret Booth QC (now a Dame), Judith Hughes and Mary Hogg, Lord Hailsham's daughter were some of the other practising barristers in those chambers at the time. They were extremely helpful to me, the newcomer pupil.

Pupillage is the practical way of learning how a barrister goes about preparing for his or her cases. Just to give you a taste of what a day in pupillage is like: on one day, I went to the City and Mayor of London's Court where Paul had been involved in a case for several days and where the judge was giving his summary. Paul asked me to write up the summary and then come back to chambers for a long conference. We didn't always finish at the same time; it depended on what had to be done for the next day. I was sent to various courts to watch the proceedings in which Paul Focke was involved.

He was an able speaker and it was fascinating being his pupil. I sat in on many conferences with clients and went over to the High Court to make applications for this and that. My own long-lasting family court case aided me enormously. George and I had been through a lot of the nitty-gritty preparation for the hearings over the years and pupillage not only showed me we had done a reasonably good job, but I knew first-hand the things that needed to be done, which other pupils might not have come across before. This stood me in good stead.

During my time with Paul, in January 1979, we celebrated Lord Denning's, 80th birthday. He was the Master of the Rolls and crowds of lawyers trooped into his court to wish him well. There was hardly room for all of us to stand. He'd given orders that there were to be no speeches, but the atmosphere of goodwill towards him was tangible. Afterwards, Paul went into Dame Margaret Booth's Court. She was now a High Court judge and Paul made an application to have the case we were engaged on, heard by another judge. There was an obscure technical reason for the request. She refused the application, and so the next day we went in front of His Honour Judge Ellison. He agreed to have the hearing transferred to another judge. All this was in a day's work, but I enjoyed my six months with Paul Focke and learnt a lot from him.

Most of the time I was a dogsbody running around for my pupil master, but occasionally I was being treated like a VIP. For instance, I was contracted to do some revoicing work on the Bond film *Moonraker* and Paul allowed me to interrupt the pupillage to pop over to the Paris studios where they made a big fuss of me.

Days after I finished my pupillage with Paul, Sir George Baker contacted me again and asked me to marshal with him in the High Court.

Sir George said the case would last for two weeks. He was sitting in the Family Division of the High Court and I joined him on the bench. Having spent years making submissions before Sir George from the body of this very court, I now found myself beside him, looking down on the proceedings. Remembering how nervous I had been during all those years when I was a litigant in person, it was strange viewing the court from above.

The case before us concerned Astrid Proll, a former member of the Baader-Meinhof gang who had fled the German courts while waiting to give evidence. The Baader-Meinhof gang – or Red Army Faction as it later became known – was a German left-wing urban guerrilla group. It was responsible for killing more than 30 people during a campaign which started in the late 1960s. Proll entered the UK using a passport which she had obtained in the name of Senta Sauerbier, and married Robin Puttick under that name. The German authorities discovered her true identity and location, and applied to extradite her. She applied under section 6 of the British Nationality Act 1948. That part of the Act gave an apparently unqualified right to any woman married to a UK citizen to be registered as a citizen of the United Kingdom. She sought a declaration that the marriage was a valid and subsisting marriage, as she had acquired a domicile of choice in England.

Sir George had said he wanted me to confer with him in this case as the applicant was German. He wanted me to interpret exactly what was being said. I wondered whether this was necessary as an official interpreter was in court, so wasn't that enough? He replied that he trusted me and wanted me to tell him precisely what was being said throughout. This was a significant case and it lasted for two weeks. It was the first time that I had ever seen armed police on the roof of the High Court and when we approached Sir George's rooms inside the court, there were armed police patrolling at each end of the corridors as well.

Sir George had said to me during the various hearings that he would find a legal way to prevent her from acquiring British citizenship. She had been part of a violent gang and he was determined not to grant her application. Sir George said she was a fugitive from justice and had entered the UK by the fraudulent production of an invalid passport. He cited the case of Dicey & Morrs in which it states that '… a domicile of choice cannot be acquired by illegal residence. The reason for this rule is that a court cannot allow a person to acquire a domicile in defiance of the law which that court itself administers'. This is part of the British Nationality Act 1948. The judge gave a brilliant summing up of the case and finished it by refusing the application by way of quoting a legal principle that 'No man can take advantage of his own wrong', substituting 'woman' for 'man' at the end of his decision. I was particularly fortunate in being part of the proceedings in this famous case.

For interested legal minds, this case is reported as Puttick -v- Attorney-General and Another, Family Division 1980.

It also was the start of a long and happy friendship with Sir George. We saw a great deal of each other, we went to the Royal Academy and saw various exhibitions there, and we dined out together quite frequently. I remember one memorable day when we celebrated our birthdays. He took me to a stunning restaurant called The Bell Inn at Aston Clinton in Buckinghamshire. We talked of many things that day and I remember him saying how grateful he was that he and I had become such good friends.

I jokingly remarked that he had said some rotten things about me in the summing up of my ex-husband's application for access and custody. He looked me steadily in the eyes and said, "Nikki, I didn't know you then." We went on to talk about the case and he did say that had he known me then, he would have given me custody of the children and probably not brought in the Official Solicitor. However, he also said that diplomatically, when summing up a case, while letting the deserving person win, a judge must give the losing party some comfort and this is sometimes done by praising the losing party and faintly damning the winner. Had he done this with me? "Only partly," was the answer. He smiled and we changed the subject.

Not everyone is lucky enough to have the same experience of marshalling that I had, but it does give a unique bird's-eye view of how the legal system works. My experiences were invaluable and if any budding barristers are reading this, I can't stress enough how useful it is to marshal with a judge. Apart from anything else, you will not forget the experience and it will stand out on your CV.

Shortly after the Astrid Proll case ended, I began my second pupillage at Fountain Court in the Middle Temple. The idea was that I should do my first pupillage in a Family Law Chambers and the second one in a Common Law Chambers. I wanted a thorough grounding in both aspects of the Law. So this was a Common Law Chambers. Mark Potter accepted me as a pupil and he was very helpful to me. He was charismatic and extremely knowledgeable.

I was fortunate enough to have had my application to do a *stage* in Brussels accepted. Only 220 students were taken out of 1200 applicants. There are two courses a year, one from February to July and the other from September to February. I had applied for the five-month September 1979 course.

This was due to start during the Fountain Court pupillage. I thought it would be hard to persuade Mark Potter to let me go for five months, to take up the scholarship. However, he was encouraging and said he thought it would be good for me. He warned me that he would probably not be able to be my pupil master on my return as he was going to 'take silk', which means to be appointed as a Queen's Counsel (QC, a senior barrister) and would be unable to take pupils. Indeed, he went on to become a high court judge, president of the Family Division and head of Family Justice from 2005-2010 and a Lord Justice of Appeal from 1996-2010, quite apart from many other prestigious appointments, as befits someone of his calibre.

So when I returned from Brussels after the *stage*, my new pupil master was Michael Lerego, a gentle and kindly barrister who was extremely good at getting the best out of people. He has also become a QC since then and I remember him with great affection, as I do Mark Potter.

Barrister, 1978

CHAPTER 16
AT THE HEART OF THE EEC

George and I arrived in Brussels on 10th September 1979 and I went to see Herr Wolfgang Kraus who was the administrator for the *stagiaires*. We all needed a place to stay for the duration of the *stage* and he took us to see his assistant, Rosabel. She was helping the *stagiaires* find accommodation for the five-month internship. She gave me three addresses, but only one was within walking distance of the Berlaymont, the building where I would be based.

This was a large town house in Avenue Michel-Ange. I rang the front door bell and a face peeped at me from around the front door. It was a cross between Charles Trenet and Edward Heath. He said "Oui?" in a high-pitched voice and I explained that I was doing a *stage* at the Berlaymont and needed to rent a room for the time I was there. He invited me in and told me he was Richard, pronounced 'Reeechar' and his partner's name was Raoul de Manez, first name pronounced Raoool, with the emphasis on the second syllable. He took us on a grand tour of the 'maison', taking pains to point out the features of special interest. The grande salle was large and imposing and contained an ancient clavichord, but the pièce de résistance was the painting of the Countess de Manez, Raoul's mother. He was an actor and inherited the house after his mother died. The house was reminiscent of a stage set. I was shown downstairs, where there was a bar and sitting area leading on to the garden. The décor was interesting; the walls were bright red and the sofa was covered in fur. But there was an awful lot of dust! However, the atmosphere was decadently irresistible.

Richard led us up the ornate staircase and he showed me an available room at the top of the house, overlooking the garden. He told me that the bureau and bed were ancient and valuable. The room was very large with a marble fireplace and an ornate sofa which turned into a bed. The furniture was old and rather endearing, waiting to be polished and lived in. I think my daughter Kerry, who had since begun work in the hotel industry, would have used the trade jargon 'tired'. A large gold and silver framed mirror stood on the mantelpiece and a marble table was arranged with two warm and cosy green velvet armchairs waiting to embrace us. Into this old world tranquillity there was juxtaposed a white plastic modern desk with a bright yellow desk lamp and a red steel chair with a black tie-on cushion. These must have belonged to the last tenant as they certainly did not fit into the general faded elegance of the room. The desk faced a new white partition wall behind which was the kitchen and a bath and shower room. The dining table was made of wood with gabled legs and four beautiful matching chairs, but they needed re-covering. The window had a large marble sill which overlooked Raoul and Richard's patio, and the secluded pretty garden backing on to a church.

Because of the atmosphere that the house engendered, the comical mannerisms of Richard – who obviously adored his Raoul – and Raoul, whose stage life had entered and permeated the décor, plus the view from my window, I made the decision to take the room. We were to meet this famous classical actor the next day, when he was to play the part of Egmont in the Grand Place as part of the Brussels millennium celebrations.

George and I slept in the room that night. It was handsome as aforesaid, but as far as we were concerned, its charms did not extend to the thick layer of dust and balls of fluff that gently wafted backwards and forwards every time the breeze caught them. Something had to be done, so we decided to spring clean the room, even though it was autumn.

The whole house reminded me of the film *Great Expectations*. Surprisingly, I didn't see any creepy crawlies at all. But one thing I was very particular about was having a toilet nearby. Alas, this was not to be and I had to walk down two flights of stairs to go to the loo. This was a major concession on my part to stay in the house.

The next morning, on the way down to the loo, I was stopped by Richard and Raoul's poodle – of course it had to be a poodle. She was a sweet little dog called Zinzie but had a ferocious bark. She bounded out of their room, the door of which was kept permanently wide open, so she could come and go as she pleased. I sat down on the stairs and she got on my lap for a cuddle. I was gently petting and talking to her when Raoul came out of his room. He was stark naked. He looked at me and said "oh hello" in French and went on down the stairs to the toilet without turning a hair. I let him pass and I waited my turn to go to the loo. I had not expected my first meeting with one of Belgium's foremost actors to be *au naturel*.

Sometime during the day, I wanted to make some telephone calls so I knocked on Raoul's door. His phone was on a long flex which stretched from the ground floor up to his and Richard's room on the first. This was the only phone in the house. He handed me the phone, but once again he was naked. I suppose he thought that being an actress I was used to the intimacy of stage dressing rooms and as his home was his theatre I would be able to accept his nudity. He had a fine body so I had no complaints.

George and I had been cleaning my room all day and at 6.30 that evening Raoul came to the door. This time he was dressed. He wore a black velvet suit and looked every inch the archetypal actor. He told us he was on his way to the Grand Place and if we wished we could go and see him as *Egmont*. It was going to be a great spectacle in the square and there would be a reception afterwards with the press in attendance. The next day would see the reception at his house with a King and Queen and a Countess present. We finally finished cleaning the room at ten in the evening, so we were quite late getting to the Grand Place. We arrived just as Raoul was declaiming on the subject of liberty before being executed. There were hundreds of people in the square and the spotlights were cleverly aimed not just at the stage but at the ancient buildings behind to give a majestic atmosphere to the play. We wished we had been there earlier. It felt very strange to think that this man, whom the large crowd was clapping and cheering, was indeed the same man who had introduced himself to me in the nude on the stairs, on the way to the toilet that very morning!

After the performance we returned to the house. I let several people in by the front door who had arrived saying they were waiting for Richard. I showed them in to the grand reception room and a few minutes later Richard came back with more people. He invited me and George to the bar for a drink, so we accepted. There was a large picture of a nude lady and also one of a nude man in pride of place hanging over the bar. The room had a feeling of 1930's charm but also of debauchery.

Richard and Raoul had a ménage of gay friends and we all got on well. Over the next five months I was living there I was allowed to become part of the 'family'. I was asked to join them in the red furnished fluffy room that only their special friends could enter. I witnessed some hilarious moments when their friends came to visit. One day a man called Jacques Roland came to the front door and he had his cat with him, on a lead. Both Richard and Raoul were out, but he came in anyway saying he would wait for them. He went into the main drawing room which was on the ground floor. Jacques then kneeled down on the lavishly cushioned couch and kissed it. He said it was because it had belonged to his friend, the Countess, and she had sat on that couch. Another time, two women appeared at the front door asking for donations. To them, the house was representative of aristocratic wealth and luxury and these two ladies came to try and raise money for their cause. The cause they were supporting was The Movement Against Materialism.

A week after George and I arrived in Brussels I embarked on my internship at the EEC.

To begin with, there was a reception held for the new intake of *stagiaires*. We were welcomed by Herr Wolfgang Kraus who explained that the *stagiaires* needed a committee because they would be responsible for arranging events for the months we would be there. The committee consisted of a president and five members. There would be elections in a week's time and candidates would have to make a speech, after which the *stagiaires* would vote. Whoever had the most votes would be the president and have a special role to fulfil, such as inviting speakers and initiating interesting events for the *stagiaires* to attend.

Someone put my name forward for me to be on the committee, so I thought 'why not?' It would be a way of meeting my fellow *stagiaires*. George said he would stay with me till after the vote was counted and the result was known.

My days were crowded with all sorts of social activities. It had started that first day with Raoul's performance in the Grand Place. Although this was quite separate from the internship, it was familiar to me because it was show business. The other folk we met were from different walks of life. We didn't need to buy much food as we were being invited for dinner and drinks on a daily basis!

One memorable character reminded me of Orson Welles in his later years. The resplendently named Marcus Aurelius Cogbill was an outsized American property salesman, based in Brussels but selling plots of land in Florida. According to him that would be the next Shangri-La and the opportunity to get in on a good deal should not be missed. He later relocated to London and we were able to go on seeing him there. He would invite us to his big rented house on the River Thames and ply us with generous helpings of his home-cooked spaghetti. I met Marcus through his secretary, Sue and she was often accompanied by her Dutch friend, Benno. He was a habitual drug taker and excused it by demonstrating with pinched fingers that the amount he took was 'like so, a little bit'.

I was aware that I had to make a good speech for the *stagiaire's* committee. I worked long and hard to make it sound persuasive. The day arrived and I felt the timetable for the events was designed to make me more nervous than I already was! First there was a lecture, which I was only half listening to, then we all had coffee and only after that came the speeches. There were 13 altogether. We were called in alphabetical order and my name came 11th on the list. I made my speech partly in German and French, as well as English.

Mr Kraus came over to me afterwards and said in German, "That was a very effective speech you made," but I was eager to find out who had been elected. There was a cocktail party in the evening and it was not till then that Rosabel read out the names of people who had been voted onto the committee. I had 112 votes and tied with Charles, one of the friends I had met a few days earlier. We got the top votes and shared joint presidency of the committee.

George was pleased at my success, bought me flowers and was lovely as usual. It was great having him there, but I missed seeing my children, Kerry and Darrell. Thank goodness for the telephone as I could still keep in touch and hear their news. It wasn't the same thing as being with them, but it helped and I made the journey back across the channel as often as I could. George now had to go home and I was sorry to see him leave.

The next few days were a blur of meeting other *stagiaires*, organising the whole student committee and finding a place to meet. Eventually committee rooms on the ground floor of the Berlaymont were allocated to us.

There we all met for the first time, a getting to know you session. We got on very well with each other and with the commissioners. I must explain that this was a kind of Students' Union, but not like a university one, as in the UK, where they are just about tolerated. In the EEC, we were much respected and our opinions were sought on all kinds of matters. What a contrast, to be so appreciated.

In my speech I had talked about the various events I planned for the term and now we on the committee had to put together some of those events for real. We organised a lot of parties and dances, which proved very popular in the first couple of weeks and allowed the *stagiaires* to meet socially. I prepared dinner parties in my room and Richard came and met some of my friends too.

We organised other more serious events also. One was a trip to Berlin. This we did at the end of October 1979. We were a jolly group and were accompanied by Madam Aufrecht. We did all the interesting things, like seeing and going into the Gedenkniskirche, the church that was bombed out in the Second World War and has been kept in its mangled, damaged state. Gedenknis means remembrance and we visited the memorial stones in Berlin-Spandau and the Berlin Wall. I had seen all these sights previously when I visited Berlin with George for the first time in 1971, but I was now seeing them through the trainees' eyes. They all knew and had read about the Wall, but seeing it for real, with guards looking out and holding their rifles, knowing they would use them if they felt it necessary, was quite a different story and left us all feeling chilled to the bone. We were also shown over the Reichstag building.

As I spoke German, I was asked to interpret for our group, which felt completely weird, considering that I might have been a victim of the policy to destroy all the resident Jews, had I remained in Berlin. What a horrible history. Many years later, a young friend I was visiting in Frankfurt said how ashamed he was to be German and how difficult it was not to be able to be proud of his history. None of the Nazi horrors had anything to do with him and I felt sorry that Germany's legacy made him feel this way. So Hitler not only murdered a whole generation, but also destroyed any pride future generations could feel for their recent history and homeland.

There were also several visits to the coffee houses on the Kurfürstendamm, which were warm and welcoming places after the bleak history we had been taking in. One café there had been regularly visited by Gert Fröbe, my *Goldfinger* friend and they made a big feature out of that.

We also took the *stagiaires* to Strasbourg, one of the places where the Parliament sits.

Apart from arranging trips to places of interest and relevance to the trainees, the committee also planned special events such as asking well-known dignitaries to speak to the *stagiaires*. On one occasion a certain Monsieur Chirac, who was then a commissioner at the EEC, came to speak to us.

As president of the *stagiaires* I had to meet him and bring him into the room where we met. We spoke in French together and I must have made a good impression on him, because after chairing the meeting, on the way back to his office, he asked me to join his 'cabinet'. I would have loved to accept his offer, but I had a husband and children in London and explained that it was impossible for me to take up his invitation. I was very flattered that he thought so highly of me. He was a very good and entertaining speaker and he went down very well with the *stagiaires*. Later, he would rise to become President of France from 1995 to 2007. Unfortunately, he blotted his copy book and in 2011 was given a two-year suspended prison sentence for diverting public funds and abusing public trust.

Another interesting speaker we were fortunate to get was General Joseph (Joe) Luns, Secretary-General of NATO from 1971-1984. This was four years after the American war in Vietnam and there was still much criticism of their involvement. He talked to us about the different aspects of the war. He also clarified his role in NATO, which he said was one of great influence and a crucial one.

Roy Jenkins was the President of the European Commission at that time and the first Briton to hold that post. I would see him walking along the corridors of the Berlaymont and he reminded me of the comic French film character, Monsieur Hulot, whose trousers ended above his ankles and did a funny lurching walk. Jenkins' term was primarily remembered for reviving the idea of European monetary union. Look at the disaster that policy has proved to be!

There were 28 European Commission departments called Director Generals (DGs), including the legal one, to which I was attached. Our department dealt with EEC legislation. I worked for Herr Ficker who was referred to, in the French style, as my *adviser*. The work concerned international markets, legislation for consumers, industrial affairs, freedom of establishment, freedom to provide services and the Passport Union, but many different subjects arose under those headings. Reports came in every day from various departments and I had to analyse them.

My ability to speak German came in useful as Herr Ficker was German, but the first language of the EEC was French. English was supposed to be equal with French within the organisation, but every time I made a call to the Commission, I was spoken to in French. It became annoying, so eventually I decided to make a point of speaking only English to the operator.

I had to study the various Consumer Acts of the EEC in order to harmonise legislation for all the member states. The British Parliament had asked my adviser to examine the feasibility of an exemption of the law for the handicraft industry. The reply was that it was not possible to exclude the legislation for the UK as it was impractical.

Even then it was becoming apparent to me that the EEC harboured ambitions beyond its stated purely economic union, and was angling for total political union as its ultimate goal. It came home to me in the way the legislation was being drafted. It seemed to me that the idea was to merge all the countries into a single state. I felt if this were to be achieved then the essential characteristics of the countries would be lost. They would be moulded into a monolith ruled over by the EEC. Unfortunately, my instinct was correct. In my opinion, the current European Union has fulfilled its erstwhile ambition to dominate the whole of Europe. The EU still offers internships as a way of creating a cohort of 'goodwill ambassadors' for European ideas and values.

A more pleasant aspect of the EEC environment for me was the existence of a theatre group which performed Shakespeare's plays and was popular with many of the English officials.

One day a woman called Midge phoned to ask if I would play Maria in their forthcoming production of *Twelfth Night*. Someone must have told her about my theatrical background. I felt very flattered to be asked. The next day I went to the first rehearsal which took place in the International Language Centre. I liked the members of the group and the feelings seemed to be mutual. We went through the scenes and after looking at the schedule of rehearsals, I decided to take on the role.

I spent a lot of time rehearsing Maria between my work at the Berlaymont, arranging events for the *stagiaires* and coming home for the occasional weekend to be with George and the children.

The first performance took place in December 1979. I was very nervous. I hadn't been on a stage for years and now I was going to perform in front of my boss, work colleagues and fellow *stagiaires*. The local press were going to be there as well. The butterflies in my tummy didn't help. Although I always feel sick with worry before going on stage, once out in front, the nerves go and I start to enjoy the play. As it happens, the show went off very well and it was incredibly well received. Afterwards we all went back to the Corkscrew, the pub the Brits always regarded as their local, and the cast, crew and friends celebrated our success.

Things died down a bit just before Christmas and I was able to go back home and spend the holidays with Kerry, Darrell and George.

I returned to Brussels early in January 1980. For some years the theatre group had entered the annual theatrical competition which was to take place in Luxembourg. This year they decided to enter Noel Coward's play *Hands Across the Sea* and asked me to play the lead. The company had done very well in recent years, but this time we wanted to be the winners. They thought with me in the lead they stood a chance, so there was a lot resting on my shoulders. Even if the company was amateur, the performances were of a professional standard. Unfortunately, we only came second, but the company said I had done well and although I felt I had let them down, they supported me brilliantly.

I was still working in the legal department with Herr Ficker. However, I had become fascinated with the press side of things and wanted a change of scenery from the legal one. I was told that *stagiaires* had to spend their entire placement in their designated department and nobody had ever been allowed to move before. I had a word with Herr Kraus and, lo and behold, I was allowed to work part-time in the press department! This was fascinating as I had been preparing statements for the ministers' meetings in the legal department and now I was attending those meetings in a journalistic capacity. This went on for the last few weeks in Brussels and the experience would stand me in good stead later.

Inevitably, the final day of the *stage* arrived and saying goodbye to people I had become close to was sad. But all good things must come to an end and I had enjoyed my stay in Brussels immensely.

CHAPTER 17

THE WESTMINSTER VILLAGE

Being back permanently in London, I could see George and the children every day. I continued my pupillage with Michael Lerego at Fountain Court as I still had three months to go before being fully qualified as a barrister. Coming back to my chambers I was brought back to earth with a bump. Having got used to the rarefied position I had enjoyed in Brussels, I was now fetching and carrying for the barristers and making tea. I had hoped to get a permanent position in Fountain Court Chambers after my pupillage, but this was not to be.

David Mellor had been elected as a Member of Parliament for Putney in the 1979 General Election. After I returned from Brussels, he asked me to join him in the House of Commons as his assistant.

I thought long and hard about David's offer. After all, I had spent many years studying law, inspired to do so by my experiences in the High Court, battling to keep my children.

I realised that I had a talent for asking the right questions of a witness and felt excited by the atmosphere of the court. No wonder there are so many plays about courtroom dramas. As an actress, the combination of acting and delivering my own script in court fascinated me.

I also wanted to help women in a similar situation to my own. However, by the time I returned to London from Brussels, the divorce law had changed dramatically and women did not have such a raw deal in 1980 as had been the case in the 1960s. The courts were now more inclined to give custody of the children to the mothers.

I had become interested in politics when I was preparing and writing papers for discussion at EEC ministers' meetings. I had met quite a few members of the European Parliament and had got to know some of the EEC commissioners and had discussed politics with them.

After all, politics is about important issues and the various political parties represent the different opinions on those issues. I never understand how anyone can say they are not interested in politics. I know how politicians can, and do, put people off in the way they behave and jostle for position, but that takes place in so many organisations and institutions as well, and it has nothing to do with trying to solve serious issues that arise in our country and which have to be dealt with.

After much consideration of David's offer, I decided to take it. It was difficult trying to find rooms in chambers with hundreds of other young hopefuls and I thought working in the House of Commons might be more exciting than dragging my heels from one magistrates' court to another, especially in the early stages of being a junior barrister.

Although I did not continue my law career, looking back I realise how fortunate I was to get as far as I did in the profession. After achieving success as a graduate of the Bar I did not encounter any difficulties in finding pupillage. The position is rather different today. There are now far too many budding lawyers leaving law schools with limited prospects for them to begin pupillage. Some say that the law schools are too indiscriminate, allowing anyone to be admitted when they simply have no hope of a career at the Bar. This has been officially recognised and recommendations have been made for an aptitude test which will weed out those who do not have the skills or talent. Indeed, the Inns are being encouraged to give a 'health warning' to students to advise them of the challenges and difficulties that lie ahead.

I think I got as far as I did because I had actual experience in the courts, plus natural attributes derived from my drama training. Being a barrister in court does require giving a performance, to some extent. Besides, I do not think I would have been invited by so many eminent judges to be their marshal, if they did not think I had the ability to make intelligent contributions to their cases.

David Mellor was a marvellous barrister, which also made him a good MP. He is brilliant at thinking on his feet and is incredibly articulate. I have never seen him use notes during his speeches in House of Commons' debates.

It was interesting working with him. It was the time of the Unification Church, the controversial 'Moonies' sect and David's campaign to strip them of their charitable status. The point of charitable status is that they do not pay any taxes. The Charities Commission refused to do so and David castigated the Charities' Commissioner as a result. He was also involved in working on the new Criminal Justice Bill, which was extremely interesting.

The work I was doing for David was mainly research into the issues he was involved with, but I helped sort out his constituents' concerns as well. If they had a problem, they would call the office and the gamut of issues ranged from the council evicting a tenant to the fact that a plumber had not turned up. I enjoyed dealing with the public, but sometimes I found it a bit wearing.

David's office in which I worked was the Norman Shaw Building, formerly Scotland Yard, and not far from John Major's office. He was a good friend of David's and he became my friend as well. I used to go and talk to him about any problem that arose. He would listen patiently and then quietly give me his advice. We would also discuss political issues of the day that would come up.

John Major was a rare person who had been a popular Chief Whip of the Conservative Party. Whips are usually feared and hated by the MPs. The reason for this is that they can often be brutal to their party's backbenchers in order to secure their vote and will resort to a mixture of promises, threats, blackmail and extortion to force an unpopular vote. They try to find out everyone's secrets but do not always succeed as has been seen on various occasions. In fact, it was later, under John Major's own premiership that scandals both sexual and financial took on horrendous proportions. In 1992, David Mellor, now a cabinet minister was exposed as having an extramarital affair and accepting hospitality from the daughter of a leading member of the Palestine Liberation Organisation (the PLO). This was a shock to me as I was so fond of both David and his wife Judith who had helped me through my Bar finals.

Then the MP Stephen Milligan was found dead after strangling himself while performing a solitary sexual act.

John Major's own affair with Edwina Currie didn't help either, even though by the time he became PM it was over. I have never understood what attracted him to Currie. Norma Major was, in my opinion, much better looking and to my mind she was certainly a much more attractive personality.

But while John was PM there were many other scandals, including the 'Cash for Questions' affair. Neil Hamilton and Tim Smith received money from Mohamed Al Fayed to ask questions in the House of Commons. There were many other MPs involved at that time, not just in taking money to ask questions, but in arms deals with foreign countries. One MP, Jonathan Aitken, was accused of doing secret deals with leading Saudi princes. He denied the accusations, but early on in the subsequent trial it became clear he had lied under oath. He was convicted of perjury and imprisoned.

In our later journalistic contact I had no idea what he was engaged in. I found him to be a kind man who invited me and a girlfriend to spend a few days at a health farm in which he had a financial interest. We were pampered and beautifully looked after and at the end of the treatment he asked me if I would be able to write an article of appreciation of the health spa. I had no reason not to and wrote a glowing report of my experience there.

So, as I have shown, the whips cannot always keep up with their MPs' scandals and transgressions. However, MPs will sometimes tell the whips confidential things about their colleagues in order to be in the whips' good books, just like being in school and currying favour with the teacher! Whips can bribe an MP by suggesting that he or she could join the Foreign Affairs Committee, join fact-finding trips to exotic places, become chairman of a committee, or threaten to expose something about them. A good whip will use the secrets and incriminating information they have obtained about their MPs in order to force them to vote their way. So you can see why a Chief Whip would not be very popular!

Because the party whip's job is to ensure the successful outcome of a vote, there have been cases where Members of Parliament were brought in by ambulance when they were too ill to travel. This is especially so on a vote where it is crucially important for the party which holds the majority to win. They can make allowances for MPs who are away on important business, or whose political circumstances require them to take a particular single issue very seriously, or if there is a mass revolt. On one occasion I personally witnessed this when one MP had difficulty in supporting the government. Andrew Bowden was the MP for Brighton Kemptown, a constituency with a large number of retired elderly folk on pensions. The Conservatives were trying to cut public spending and one of the ways was planned legislation to abolish the heating allowances for the elderly. Well, Andrew relied on these people to retain his seat in Parliament, so voting in favour of the cuts would not only go against what he felt was right, it would also, more pragmatically, cost him his seat at the next election. Well, the whips didn't want that either, so he was excused.

Theoretically at least, expulsion from the party can be the result of an MP defying a three-line whip. The Chief Whip sends out a letter at the start of each week to all the MPs in their party with the issues to be voted on. This document informs them of the schedule for the days ahead, and includes the sentence, 'Your attendance is absolutely essential' next to each debate in which there will be a vote. This sentence is underlined once, twice or three times depending on the consequences that will be suffered if they do not turn up, hence the origin of the terms *one-line whip, two-line whip* and *three-line whip.*

There was an example of this in the case of John Major's government. Nine Conservative Members of Parliament had their whips removed after voting against the Government over its stance on the Maastricht Treaty. It was also the only time when MPs who were being whipped were cooperating with the opposite side's whips.

As shown in BBC television series like *Yes Minister* and *House of Cards,* the Chief Whip can wield a significant amount of power over the MPs in his party, including cabinet ministers, as he is seen to speak at all times with the voice of the Prime Minister.

The role of Chief Whip is regarded as secretive. He (not so far as I am aware, ever a she) is concerned with the discipline of his own party's Members of Parliament and never appears on television or radio in the capacity of whip. Whips in the House of Commons do not speak in debates. There are some cases in which whips are removed because an issue is a matter of conscience. These include adoption, religion and equal opportunities. The impact of a whip being imposed on a matter of conscience can be damaging for a party leader. One such case was that of Iain Duncan Smith who imposed a three-line whip against the adoption of children by gay couples. Several Conservative MPs voted against the official party line, and Duncan Smith's authority was thereby weakened.

When John Major became Chief Secretary to the Treasury, I wrote him a poem before the budget and a note wishing him well. He replied and said he could not have done the speech without my little rhyme. When he became Prime Minister after Mrs Thatcher's ousting, he asked me to work for him during the following election. I spent the 1992 campaign in Central Office, writing reports on how the campaign was progressing. After he won, I was invited to Number 10 to attend his garden party.

When David Mellor became a Parliamentary Private Secretary (PPS) to Francis Maude MP, it meant he had to give up his personal staff, so I could no longer work for him. He had been a good friend to me during and after my Bar finals and later on I enjoyed working in his office. I was sorry to leave him.

During my time with David I had become familiar with the workings of the House of Commons and knew many of the MPs. This was a valuable asset and not long after this, I was asked to join Television South (TVS), to work with the political editor, Brian Shallcross, in the press gallery of the House of Commons. TVS had only just been awarded the franchise over the previous company, Southern Television, and I found myself with TVS on their first day on air. They had their studios in both Maidstone and Southampton.

My new office was located next to Big Ben in the press gallery and is one of the most photographed buildings in the world. It was exciting to be there. From the windows I could see the whole of Parliament Square and watch the people rushing to and fro. Brian Shallcross was a veteran broadcaster with many years' experience of interviewing ministers and MPs. When I joined him he gave me valuable advice and guidance. Subsequently, he and his family were to become close friends of mine.

The work was varied and interesting and because we were broadcast journalists, it wasn't just a case of writing a newspaper article to a daily or weekly deadline; it was getting interviews with ministers and MPs filmed in time for transmitting that evening. A courier would come in the afternoon to pick up our items for the news at 6.00 pm. They had to be delivered to both studios, so it was essential that we finished the interviews on time. They were either done in our studio in Norman Shaw North Building, which was used as an extension of the House of Commons and where David Mellor's office was, or on the green outside the Houses of Parliament, if the weather permitted.

Each day was different and after getting to the office, we would liaise with the Southampton newsroom and they would tell us which MP from the TVS region they wanted us to interview. This would either be in connection with a news item from the area, or their point of view on an issue that affected the constituency. We then had to try to find the MP or minister, which was not always easy. There was a tannoy system in the press gallery, but no such thing existed around the Commons building. They were still living in the nineteenth century. If one needed to contact an MP, you had to approach the Sergeant at Arms and he would take a silver platter bearing a card with the MP's name around the building trying to find him or her. Some of the venues that might be visited included the many bars that exist in the House! That would take precious time and even when the person was found, we had to haggle about the timing of the interview. He or she might be in a meeting and couldn't make the interview, so we would have to change the plan to suit everyone. Then, having done that, we would have to find the TV crew and make sure they were free to shoot the interview. Often they were busy at that time and we would have to start all over again. It was seat-of-your-pants stuff and often became stressful. You never knew if you would get the items ready in time. I used to come home exhausted and George would revive me.

After a few years, I was privileged to become a lobby correspondent. This is not to be confused with a person who is a lobbyist. A lobbyist is an activist who is usually paid by an interest group to promote their positions in Parliament. On the other hand, a lobby correspondent is a journalist, one of a relatively small group of accredited journalists who enjoy privileged access to Government spokespeople. They are allowed into the Members' Lobby, which is how they got their name. They are able to talk in private to MPs and ministers and also meet the Prime Minister's press officer regularly. They are well informed about what is going on in Parliament, but they usually keep their sources of information confidential. The job of lobby correspondent is over 100 years old. It first started in 1884, when Parliament passed a motion allowing one gentleman of the press (*The Times*) to go into the Members' Lobby. The lobby system grew from there. Unfortunately, all the records from those early days were lost in 1941 when the House of Commons was bombed during the Blitz. The lobby was not allowed to see the PM's spokesman until the 1926 General Strike. In the 1920s and 1930s, meetings were sporadic and it was only after 1945 that they became a regular feature.

When Mrs Thatcher was Prime Minister, we, the lobby, crowded into Number 10 Downing Street every morning and her press secretary, Bernard Ingham, used to take the briefings. These consisted of giving us the PM's movements for the day and giving her opinions on current matters. We would ask questions about issues that were often controversial. Bernard always spoke in the plural 'we think that etc...' and this was Mrs T. speaking. He identified with her so closely that you felt she was speaking through him, which in reality she was. These briefings are not attributable, so we went to meetings that never officially took place. There was some criticism of the lobby system and when I was in the House, *The Guardian* and *Independent* newspapers were not part of the lobby. The problem, as they saw it, was that it was merely a propaganda exercise, but that is not what the lobby briefings are about. Ministers will often give their favourite journalists exclusive stories, which is also not ethical, so it is better to have an organised system where everyone has the same briefing. And anyway, any journalist worth his or her salt gets the opposing views before publishing. However, Bernard's briefings were only a part of the lobby system. There is a social extension system to the lobby which probably still exists today.

Apart from the No. 10 briefings, there are lobby briefings in the press gallery in the afternoon, but we also got to meet the MPs and ministers in the numerous bars of the House, the main one being Annie's Bar. It is so called because she was the first barmaid, but she's long since gone to that great bar in the sky! She was succeeded by an ex-RAF sergeant with a large moustache. MPs of different political parties may have their differences on the floor of the House, but it is surprising how famously they get on when they mingle with each other in the bar. For example, the Rt. Hon. Robert Rhodes James, the historian and booklover and left-wing Labour MP, Eric Heffer, used to talk together as old friends, as well as Norman St John Stevas. Eric was a fanatic book collector. His lovely wife Doris said he could never pass a bookshop without going in. His collection was overflowing in their home and so one day when the abandoned church next door was up for sale, he bought it so that he would have a place to store more books. Maybe that is what drew them all together. It was stimulating to hear them discussing the books they were reading and other intellectual matters. It was fascinating listening in on their conversations.

Brian and I would talk to our area MPs in the bars about various matters they were interested in and when the subject merited it, we would invite them to be interviewed for the Sunday political program on TVS, which was an in-depth discussion of the past weeks' subjects.

When a print journalist wrote about a breaking story in the next day's newspapers which included the words 'from a reliable source', it may well have come from a conversation with an MP in Annie's Bar. One day I went into the bar and Eric, who was always the life and soul of the party, was sitting, looking morosely into his glass. I asked him what was bothering him and he told me he had just been diagnosed with terminal cancer. I was devastated at the news. The place wouldn't be the same without him. He did rally and as he was writing his book at the time, he swore cheekily that he would 'get' Tony Blair from beyond the grave. This was before Blair had become known to the wider public but was already a thorn in the side of the old Labour stalwarts. I used to visit Eric in his London flat and he would show me the latest additions.

Sitting upstairs in the press gallery in the chamber of the House of Commons during debates and PMs' Questions was always interesting. We saw a different side of the MPs, especially the ones we got to know from our area. Question Times were particularly interesting. They used to take a quarter of an hour on Tuesdays and Thursdays when I was there, but Tony Blair later changed that to half an hour on Wednesdays. These are occasions when the Opposition tries to embarrass the Prime Minister by catching him or her unawares. Mrs Thatcher was rarely caught out and John Major got used to the unexpected question. Whereas previous PMs used a notebook to answer questions, Tony Blair did it off the cuff.

The Prime Minister never knows what the opposition MPs will ask. There used to be two questions, the first one innocuous and the second one with the sting in it. At the beginning of the week the MPs' names are all put in a hat and names are drawn out first, second and third etc. They are the lucky ones who will be asking the PM questions. If the MP asking the question is from the PM's own party, they will have disclosed their question. The PM can then prepare an appropriate answer. If the MP doesn't know what to ask, the PM might put forward an idea on which the PM needs to know how the House will respond. A problem usually arises when an Opposition member is going to ask the PM a question. This was so daunting for Harold McMillan when he was Prime Minister that he was physically sick with nerves every Tuesday and Thursday, not knowing what questions he would have thrown at him. Harold Wilson would spend many a lunchtime looking up the interests of the MPs opposing him, to try and guess what they would ask.

Eric Heffer told me what happened when he had a go at Mrs Thatcher one Question Time. He had asked her when she was coming to Liverpool, his constituency. She said she had no plans to do so. He became annoyed and told her, in no uncertain terms, that she should come as there were problems that he wanted her to address. He told me he had sat down and almost immediately regretted the way he had spoken to the Prime Minister. At the end of the session, he wanted to see her and saw Ian Gow, one of TVS's MPs and Margaret Thatcher's PPS coming down the stairs.

Ian Gow was a lovely man and tragically, in 1990 he was murdered when the IRA planted a bomb under his car. He was supposed to check everything before he got in his car, according to the security guidelines, but he was easygoing and didn't bother. That cost him his life and we were all in shock, especially Mrs Thatcher who had lost a good friend.

Anyway, Eric said he wanted to see Maggie and Ian told him that she wanted to see him! He explained to me that whenever one was summoned to the Prime Minister, they were always terrified as she was not slow to come forward with her remarks. Well, he arrived at her office and was about to apologise when she said something like, "No Eric, I want to say something first. I want to say you were quite right about Liverpool and I'm sorry I haven't been yet." Eric said he nearly fell off his chair. I must say I laughed while he was telling me all this. I was imagining Eric sitting in the chair like a naughty schoolboy and Mrs Thatcher, like his headmistress standing over him. Eric then said how sorry he was that he had been rude to her and she said it didn't matter. Maggie told him she would arrange to come to the constituency as soon as possible and he should take her round the problem areas. He then said something amazing. He said he fell in love with her at that moment, not sexually you understand but with her charisma. She gave him 20 minutes of her time and he stressed that she normally only gave a quarter of an hour to her own MPs. She suggested that he should exit by the back stairs so as not to be seen by his party's members coming from her office. So my left-wing friend fell in love with his right-wing Prime Minister! What a hoot.

During my time in the House, the issue of televising Parliament came up. It was only recorded for radio in those days, and listening to PM's Questions the next morning, it was difficult to realise I had been in the chamber for the event as it sounded quite different. There were microphones in the roof which picked up the general sound, plus the MPs' individual microphones which came on when each MP began to speak and which distorted the voice. Television would change all that because the UK, at that time, was one of the few democracies that didn't have TV broadcasts of Parliament's daily happenings. Many people (then) got their information from TV and it was ludicrous simply to show a still photo of the politician on the evening news with a recording of what he or she had said. There was plenty of opposition to having the cameras in the chamber at the time. The benches, on which the MPs sat, had built-in loudspeakers at the back of the seats so they could hear what was going on. To help them concentrate, MPs would sometimes sit back and close their eyes. Those opposing the televising of Parliament said this might look to the viewers as though the Member was asleep. Another reason was that often the chamber would look empty and the conclusion might be drawn that nobody was interested in being there. However, the reality was that during debates, Members might be elsewhere, attending important meetings in the Select Committees, discussing proposed legislation, or seeing constituents. Anyway, we have had the cameras in the Houses of Parliament for several years now, so those arguments have been overridden. Now more and more folk can watch PM's Questions, which for many is the showpiece of Parliament.

As I indicated it is the Select Committees that do the most effective work of the House. Select Committees work in both Houses. There are from 10 to 15 Members in a committee. They check and report on areas ranging from the work of government departments to economic affairs. The committee rooms are in the committee corridor and made up of Members from all sides of the House. When a proposal has been passed for legislation, it has to be scrutinised and put into a form of words (a Bill) which will then be debated on the floor of the House. It's at this point that several Members from every Party are selected to discuss the Bill. The merits of the Bill are not discussed there; that is the function of debates in the House. These meetings are open to journalists.

I was at the Conservative Party conference in 1983 when the scandal of Cecil Parkinson's extramarital affair broke. He was then Secretary of State for Trade and Industry. His lover, former secretary Sara Keays, revealed to *The Times* newspaper that she was pregnant with his child and criticised his behaviour towards her. Mrs Thatcher stood by Parkinson, but the furore in the media made it impossible for her to sustain this position, and a few days later she did accept his resignation. Every news bulletin mentioned the scandal at the time. Brian Shallcross and I had befriended him at the conference as he seemed to be ostracised. When I got back to the Commons after the conference, I was walking down the corridor when Cecil approached me, looking quite sad and he asked me if I would have dinner with him that evening. I felt sorry for him and agreed. After work I met him and we went to a small Italian restaurant near Victoria station. The place was crowded with the usual hubbub of voices and so on, but as we walked through, every one stopped talking and there was complete silence. Every eye was gazing at Cecil and me. They had all read about the scandal and were obviously wondering who in Heaven's name I was. The Maitre D' came up to Cecil and offered us a secluded table in a corner of the restaurant away from those staring eyes. Cecil explained that I was a journalist and had come to do a story. I felt completely exposed and embarrassed by the whole thing. I'd only come because I was sorry at the way he had been treated at the Tory Party conference. Now, I wished I was somewhere else.

The most infamous Conservative Party conference was the one in Brighton in October 1984 when the IRA tried to kill Mrs Thatcher and her entire Cabinet. My colleague Brian and I had come to cover the event, as we did for all the party conferences. We were staying at the Metropole Hotel, right next door to the Grand Hotel, where the Prime Minister was staying with her Cabinet. I unpacked and attended the various parties that the regional TV stations were giving for the journalists. I said hello to our then TVS boss, Greg Dyke and Mike Gatward, his assistant, before going out to dinner with our local MPs and their wives. We went back to our rooms in the hotel after midnight and I fell asleep quickly. The next day I went over to the Conference Centre and saw some of the TVS MPs, plus the well-known names at the time: Denis Thatcher, Nigel Lawson, John Butterfill and David

Mitchell. We did a few interviews and later took one or two of our MPs out for dinner.

In the early hours of the morning there was a huge explosion. The sound was phenomenally scary. Naturally, we wondered what had happened. We soon learned that a bomb had exploded at 2.54 am in the Grand Hotel. It was 12th October. Suddenly, the guests from the Grand were walking over to the Metropole for refuge. What we didn't know at the time, and the police only told us later, was that a second bomb had been planted in the Metropole. The bombers were anticipating that the guests would go to the Metropole after the initial explosion, but thank goodness that bomb never went off. People we had seen hours earlier were wandering around looking completely lost and confused. Secretary of State Keith Joseph was in his underwear looking shocked, as we all were. We saw Norman Tebbit coming out of the wreckage. Mrs Thatcher was alright, but John Wakeham, who was Parliamentary Treasury Secretary, was seriously hurt and his wife Rebecca was killed. The bomb killed five MPs, but failed to kill any of Thatcher's government ministers. The other people killed by the blast were MP Anthony Berry, Eric Taylor and Jeanne Shattock. Several more, including Margaret Tebbit (the wife of Norman), who was then President of the Board of Trade, were left permanently disabled.

Margaret Thatcher had still been awake and working on her conference speech for the following day in her suite. The bomb left her bathroom badly damaged, but luckily her sitting room where she was writing was not affected, nor was her bedroom. Both she and Denis were uninjured. She was then taken out by the back of the hotel and driven to Brighton police station. From there they were taken on to Sussex Police Headquarters at Lewes, where they stayed for the rest of the night. Next morning, at around 4.00 am, when she appeared outside the police station, she gave an impromptu interview to the BBC's John Cole. She insisted that the conference would go on as usual. Marks and Spencer were persuaded to open early at 8.00 am so that those who had lost their clothes in the bombing could replace them. Mrs Thatcher later went from the conference to visit the injured at the Royal Sussex County Hospital.

The IRA claimed responsibility the next day.

Maggie gave her speech at the end of the conference. The atmosphere in the Conference Centre was electric. As she came onto the platform, the cheering started. They cheered her all through her speech, which she had changed to a rallying cry for us all to stand together against terrorism to which we would never succumb. The cheering seemed to go on forever.

Before, during and after her speech when she left the platform, it just didn't stop. I had been to many party conferences, but this was the weirdest, most horrific, but most amazingly uplifting one after the event, ever.

Mrs T. came out of the whole episode very well. Her popularity had been waning due to her cuts to benefits including heating allowances, as discussed earlier, and the means tests for people on welfare. However, with her reaction to the IRA bombers, she suddenly became as popular as she had been during the Falklands War. She was seen to be Churchillian in the way she had remained cool and refused to submit to terrorism.

CHAPTER 18
LOSING DAD AND MEETING NEW RELATIVES

1984 was a memorable year for me in many other ways. For some time George had wanted to take me to Australia to introduce me to his family whom he hadn't seen for 20 years. But, I was still working in the House of Commons and could only take a fortnight's holiday. My boss, Bob Southgate, had not authorised my leave and it had not been officially approved, but my colleague Brian said he would cover for me. So we went ahead and booked our flights for 14th April.

The Leo Baeck College had started a Cultural Society and I was part of the committee who steered it. It was launched at the beginning of April with the idea that we would have concerts, painting exhibitions and drama events as part of the cultural activity of the college as a whole. The launch took place on 1st April and during the week I was working at the House of Commons, so it was only on the following Sunday that I wrote and told my parents about it. For some reason I was keen to let them know as soon as possible and as the post took three to four days to get to Mallorca, I was so impatient that I telephoned them in the evening and spoke to Dad. He was pleased to hear from me and I told him all the news. After I put the phone down I realised I'd left something out, so I phoned again and Dad laughed and said I must have come into some money to keep phoning. (Calls abroad cost quite a bit at that time.) I must have had some inkling in wanting to speak to Dad once more, because that was the last time I actually did.

On the morning of 10th April, Mum phoned to say that Dad had passed on in his sleep. Mum was in a state and I reassured her that I'd be with her as soon as possible. I called Sydney Pettle, the beadle who had worked alongside my dad for many years at West London Synagogue, and told him what had happened. He immediately said he would accompany me to Mallorca and do what was needed for Dad. We called Kerry and Darrell and our rabbi and other people who had to be informed, like close friends and my colleague, Brian at the House. We managed to get a flight over at 5.15 pm that afternoon, and I met Sydney at Heathrow airport. There was a slight problem as Sydney had left his passport at home, so we had to get him a temporary one. Eventually we got away and arrived at the flat in El Arenal, where my parents lived, only to be told that Dad's body had just been removed, but the hearse had broken down. Mum was a nervous person at the best of times, but right now she was in a terrible state.

Sydney was such an immense help. He had to find the people from the Jewish community in Mallorca who would perform the religious rituals of embalming and cleansing the body. This took time and that was a problem. Time was of the essence as in Jewish tradition we bury the body as soon as possible. This may be a throwback to biblical times when the heat was such that a body had to be buried quickly. However, there was another reason for haste. We had booked a flight back to Heathrow for us and Mum on Thursday, 12th April and everything had to be ready by then. We had arranged for Dad's body to be flown back to London on the Friday morning and once back in London, our Jewish community had to make arrangements before the funeral could take place that day. No funerals can be held over the Sabbath from Friday evenings to Sundays. Also, the first night of the Jewish festival of Passover was on the following Monday and no funerals can be carried out till after the festival has ended. Because George and I had our flight to Australia booked for the Saturday, the funeral had to take place before we left. This meant having it on the Friday. It seemed impossible to organise all this in time.

Luckily for us, Rabbi Hugo Gryn, the then senior rabbi at West London Synagogue and Dad's colleague before he retired, realised the difficulty and arranged for the funeral to be held on the Friday afternoon, before the Sabbath came in. We'd got back on the Thursday and spent the evening with Mum, Kerry and Darrell who all stayed the night with us. We went to Hoop Lane cemetery at 4.00 pm the next day for Dad's funeral. There had been little time to let people know about it, but even so the place was packed. The seats had been taken out of the chapel so that more people could get in. Rabbis Hugo Gryn, Lionel Blue, and Michael Leigh jointly took the service. Rabbi Jacoby, who had taken over a pulpit from Dad in Switzerland some years before and had been his student, came at short notice. As Dad's friend

Rabbi Arthur Katz arrived, so did Dad's coffin and seeing all this, I cried for the first time.

The next day, Saturday morning our family went to West London for the service and Darrell and Kerry dressed the scroll. So many friends came over to us and were supportive of Mum and all of us and expressed their affection for Dad. We heard stories of his kindness to congregants which we'd never heard before. We came home and had lunch and then George and I packed for our late evening flight to Australia.

After living in Australia for four years, George returned to London in 1964, where we met. By 1984, we had been married 16 years and he had not seen his three sisters Clarice (Clare), Eunice and Annette or brother Richard, who had all remained in Australia, for almost 20 years. We had planned to go and visit them months before but decided not to tell them as it was to be a surprise. It's just as well we didn't, as right up to the last moment, with Dad's passing, we weren't sure if we were going to be able to get away.

So that was the situation on the Saturday as we were packing to leave. Darrell drove us to the airport and had coffee with us before we boarded the plane.

It had been a frantic few days and during the long flight I had time to reflect on my relationship with my father. He was not a demonstrative man, but I felt we had a close bond. Our walks together meant we discussed many subjects, but I found it strange that he hardly ever gave a personal opinion about anything, for example the afterlife. Did he believe there was one? Dad would remark that some people thought there was such a thing and others who were sceptical. This always left me wondering what *he* himself really thought on the subject. He never praised me to my face, but years later, a friend of Dad and Mum's told me he was forever talking about me and was immensely proud of me. This came as a great surprise but also pleased me.

Dad was an active person and always wanted to help people. Having been so supportive to the Jewish community in Palma Mallorca, he fell out with the leaders of the congregation when they wanted to make it more orthodox. He had resigned earlier in the year in frustration, but had then been persuaded to come back and conduct the Seder. I found it ironic that he had died just before the festival, so maybe it wasn't meant to be.

There had been no indication that Dad was ill prior to his passing, but I believe he had become disillusioned with what he found around him. Maybe he felt life was no longer worth living. After all, 81 is not that old these days and he was a strong personality, so I feel that if he had wanted to, he could have gone on for another few years. I wrote a poem about him on the plane which came from the heart.

This was my first long-haul flight and I was glad of the chance to stretch my legs when we made a short stopover in Bombay. The next stop was Perth in Western Australia and after that we had a breathtaking view of the dawn as we flew over the arid outback and headed east to Brisbane. After so many hours on the plane we waited impatiently for our luggage. One case was damaged so we took it to the Qantas desk where we had to fill in forms for compensation. After that, to add insult to injury, the customs officials opened everything and unpacked all the presents we had bought for the family. We were not amused!

By the way, whenever I complain about the length of time it takes to fly to Australia – back then, one and a half days, at least – George always reminds me that it took five weeks by ship when he emigrated in the late '50s. From what he has told me about that – and his return trip via the Panama Canal four years later – it was probably a much more interesting way to travel.

At last we could leave the airport. We stepped out into the warm sunshine and I was immediately amazed by the colourful parrots that flew by. We hired a car for the duration of our stay and drove to a motel in Aspley, a Brisbane suburb where George's youngest sister, Annette lived with her husband, Les and son, Karl.

We didn't intend to go and see them that first evening as I had made arrangements to spend the first Seder (Passover supper) with the Jewish Reform community in Brisbane. We were invited to the home of Nancy and Henry Silver who lived in the suburb of Mount Ommaney. We had difficulty finding their house and it took us over an hour to get there. Added to which while the meal was being served, there was a power cut and we were left without light. In spite of all this, it was a warm and friendly Seder and they went out of their way to welcome us. At the end of the evening we made our way into the centre of Brisbane, strolled around, had a coffee and went back to the motel for a well-earned sleep.

The next day we went round the corner to Annette's house and knocked on the door. Eleven-year-old Karl came to open it and asked through the insect screen, who we were. When Annette recognised George's voice she came running down the stairs, screaming "George" and flung herself into his arms. That was worth the whole journey, seeing the pleasure on her face. She telephoned their mum, who lived not far away, and gently broke the news to her that George was there with me. He and I went and picked up Mum and her new husband, Fred – a retired peanut farmer – and brought them back to Annette's. Later we went over to his other sister, Clare and her husband Andy and two of their grown-up children, Jaqui and Russell and their lovely dog, Lucky.

Unbeknown to us, Annette and Les had already planned a short trip away and we readily agreed to join them. We followed their car and during the next week we explored the border country of Southern Queensland and New South Wales. We all climbed – or rather clambered – up Mount Warning, the highest peak in that region of the Great Dividing Range which was named by Captain Cook in 1770.

Halfway up the mountain, stretched across the track in front of us, from one side to the other, I encountered my first Aussie snake. It was a large carpet snake, making its way quite slowly through the undergrowth. We had lots of time to admire the olive green colour and striking cross-banding. The snake must have been around seven feet long. I had never seen a snake of that size in the wild before and was fascinated. The last part of the mountain climb was so steep, we used the chains anchored to the rock to help us up. It was quite an achievement to reach the summit and the view in all directions was stupendous. Because of its altitude it is the first place on mainland Australia to catch the sunrise each morning. Nowadays, climbing the mountain is discouraged out of respect for the local Aboriginal people for whom it has significant cultural meaning.

By the way, there is nothing to fear from carpet snakes because they belong to the python family and are non-venomous. A healthy respect is fine, however. Some homeowners like having one in their backyard because they will keep it free of rats and other vermin. But you have to be careful if you own a small pet, because – given half a chance – the snake will happily take a cat, rabbit, chicken or other appetising small mammal. If your small pet goes missing, the large bulge in the snake's body will be a clue as to where it went! Pythons are at home in the water, too. On a later visit we were standing on a footbridge over a small lake when we spotted a four to five-foot-long snake moving down the bank and entering the water. Once immersed it was a surprisingly rapid swimmer, with only its small head visible above the surface.

Other family outings included a look at Surfer's Paradise – a favourite holiday spot for locals – and on another day, a boat trip to the resort of Tangalooma on North Stradbroke Island. All the extended family came and this was a completely new experience for me, being an only child and having no family worth speaking of in England. We had our lunch on the beach close to some entertaining pelicans.

We also went to another strangely named place called Mooloolaba on the so-called Sunshine Coast. (Don't they get the same sunshine everywhere?) Along the coast is a beautiful little town called Noosa where we enjoyed the upmarket shops and individually designed waterside houses. We also loved watching the surfers and we spent time swimming in the refreshing turquoise water. Later we drove to a place called Maroochydore and went to look at the spectacular Kondalilla Falls located in a protected rainforest park. On the way back from the Falls we saw yet another carpet snake, this time a spectacular eight-foot-long specimen.

After the eye-opening and wonderful ten-day holiday we had spent exploring parts of Queensland, we said a tearful goodbye to George's mum and the rest of the family and flew back to Heathrow, via Singapore, where we had arranged to stop over for a couple of nights.

In Singapore, we did all the typical touristic things and looked around the colourful shops, where we bought some silk tops and other presents for Kerry and Darrell. We were only there two nights and decided we would indulge ourselves by having drinks in the famous Raffles Hotel bar and booked a table for an evening dinner in the lush dining room. Sitting anywhere in the hotel is quite an experience and we loved the opulence of the place. We came back later for our meal and just as an example of how posh it was, the menu had both our names printed on it. The food was delicious and we lingered long, luxuriating in the atmosphere. Finally, it was time to leave and on exiting the hotel we walked past the bar, where earlier we had enjoyed our drinks. As I looked in to the room, to my astonishment – and horror – I saw Bob Southgate, my boss, at the bar. I thought I was hallucinating, but there he was, as large as life – and he was a large man.

We hurried back to our hotel and I immediately telephoned London to speak to my colleague Brian. I asked him to find out where Bob was. He phoned back later to confirm that he was on a world tour! So that really was him in Raffles. What a million-to-one chance to see him there. I'm so glad he didn't see me!

The time we spent in Australia was much too short, given how long it takes to get there and the effects of jet lag which linger for a couple of days. I fell in love with the country, the wildlife, George's family, the people we met and the easy way of life. We determined to visit again. In fact, since that first visit,

George and I have returned nine times and for each of those trips we stayed for no less than two months. This allowed us to do a lot of exploring at a more leisurely pace. Fortunately for us, during the years we travelled, the currency exchange rate was in our favour and this afforded us the opportunity to have some wonderful Aussies experiences.

CHAPTER 19
ADVENTURES DOWN UNDER

Australia is vast – a whole continent – but such an easy place to travel around. Everyone speaks English for a start – well 'Strine' anyway. I picked up enough of the lingo to enable me to comprehend conversations which included words like chook (chicken), dunny (toilet, especially an outside one), ute (pick-up truck) and galah (stupid bird or person). Furthermore, we had the great advantage of staying, for part of our trips, with each of George's three sisters in turn. So this gave us a choice of bases to return to and recover and enjoy urban life.

Clare and Andy lived in a Queensland house raised on timber posts at Slacks Creek, south of Brisbane. This traditional style gives protection from ants and other ground insects, allows for a cooling breeze to pass under the house and provides useful storage space. They had converted one part into a snooker room and another space into basic guest accommodation. The snooker table was full size and as I love the game we made the most of the opportunity to play when staying with them. It must be said that Clare and Andy, whilst generous in having us as guests, were both a bit stingy. Well let's say careful with the pennies! The guest bedroom was so dimly lit that it made it spooky - and easier for insects to hide. We secretly purchased some high-power light bulbs and fitted them for the duration of our stay. Before we left we discreetly removed them and carefully reinstalled the dim originals.

They had a large plot of land on which Andy had cultivated a lot of different tropical fruit trees. This was the first time I had tasted a fig, freshly plucked straight from the tree. It was delicious. I was also introduced to the custard apple, and while I enjoyed the texture and taste, there were too many seeds for my liking.

I am averse to flying insects and creepy-crawlies and that is one of the downsides to Australia – or indeed any hot-climate country. But I love animals and during our various journeys I was fortunate to have seen so many native creatures in the wild. Apart from the snakes already mentioned, the list included kangaroos, wallabies, emus, koalas, crocodiles, echidna, possums, platypus, and lizards of all types and sizes. The one animal I would have loved to have seen in the wild would have been a wombat. However, I was privileged to have close contact with one handsome fellow in a wildlife park. An endangered animal which I only saw in captivity was the Tasmanian devil, during our tour of the island state of the same name, when Kerry travelled with us. Sadly, the small ferocious devil's survival is threatened by a deadly facial tumour disease.

The worst insect problems involved mosquitoes, sand flies and cockroaches. For the former I would have to apply liberal quantities of repellent and cover my arms and legs. But cockroaches were something I just couldn't handle. Our preferred way of travelling was to drive the often empty highways stopping at a convenient motel at the end of the day. It was essential that wherever we stopped they should have a swimming pool, but that was never a problem. Following a refreshing swim and a taste of the local dining we would retire to bed.

After lights out, the first indication that we had unwanted guests with us was a movement underneath the sheet, like a faint brush across our bare legs. On more than one occasion George had leapt out of bed and instructed me to lock myself into the 'secure zone' (the bathroom) and not to come out until he gave the all clear. I would hear him hunting the repellent creatures (there was invariably more than one) and the loud pounding when he dispatched one with his heavy-soled footwear. This is reminiscent of the scene in *Dr. No* when Bond terminates a tarantula spider with his shoe. After that we would try and go to sleep with the television on and all the lights ablaze, since sound and light discourages the cockies. (There you go, that's more Strine vocabulary!) I must point out that the presence of these insects was never a reflection on the establishments we stayed at. They are simply a part of tropical life and many of the motels we stayed at considerably provided a can of cockroach spray repellent in the rooms.

One creature that fascinated me was the fruit bat, also known as the flying fox. We saw them close up in captivity and they have sweet dog-like faces and ten-inch-long bodies. In the Cleveland area, where two of George's sisters moved to, there is a protected woodland alarmingly called the Black Swamp Wetlands. In fact, it is home to hundreds of nesting ibis as well as fruit bats camping out in the trees. We would often park our car across the street at dusk to watch the entertainment as the bats began to stir. They would stretch their big wings while hanging upside down and then flutter around in circles before heading off in groups to some suitable location for all-night dining. We also witnessed fruit bats flying across the Brisbane River into the city centre where they probably headed for the nectar in the botanical gardens.

There is a huge variety of birdlife down under and one of the most enjoyable sights and sounds is the parrots' evening reunion. If you are in the right spot you can watch them in their hundreds as they arrive in pairs to congregate in the branches of a favoured tree. Their loud squawking goes on for ages while they socialise and exchange gossip before settling down for the night.

One bird which I did not expect to see in the wild in Australia was the penguin; definitely a bird, even if it does not fly. On Phillip Island, south of Melbourne, we sat on specially constructed viewing stands waiting for the nightly return of the small fairy penguins. They had been fishing in the cold southern waters which extend to the Antarctic. We watched them waddle hurriedly up the beach to be greeted by their mates and then continue together to their own burrows above the shoreline. The event is called the Penguin Parade and it is very commercially organised, but not to be missed if you are down that way.

We had seen whales and dolphins both from the land and, even better, from whale-watching boat trips. It is exciting to see these magnificent mammals breaching so close up. But we knew there were other animal treasures under the water. Along Australia's east coast is the Great Barrier Reef – the world's largest marine reserve – and there is only one way to see that.

I have never liked swimming because I simply do not like getting water in my eyes. This might be because of the childhood operations to my eyes which I related in an earlier chapter. Anyway when we, including Kerry at one time, were in North Queensland, we went on a day cruise from Port Douglas to the Low Isles, a small four-acre coral cay. George (a passionate swimmer with a medal for winning first place in a swimming contest when he was 11 to prove it), knew what awaited us and insisted that we don a mask and snorkel and have a look under the surface. The instant I dipped my face into the warm waters, I was hooked (no pun intended). The sight of so many beautiful colourful fish was astounding. Thereafter we determined to see more and went on several day trips to the outer reefs. High-speed catamarans transport you to pontoons which are permanently anchored to the seabed next to the reef. From the pontoon you can swim just a few yards and see the subterranean wonderland. You don't even have to dive down, you can just float on the surface and gaze at the panorama a few feet below.

We loved the reef but were not too keen on the long two-hour trips each way to get to the outer reef from the mainland. We found a wonderful solution: the reef cruise ships which depart from Cairns and Townsville and stay at sea for four to seven days. These gave us the luxury of staying in a comfortable environment with a spacious cabin and delicious meals but mooring each day right over a different reef. Once the platform at the rear of the ship is lowered you can step straight into the water. In addition, the ships have their own small glass-bottomed boats which traverse the coral and give an alternative close-up view. The ships are relatively small, carrying only about 40 passengers and with a friendly, informative crew make it a wonderful way to understand and appreciate the reef. But not only the reef. Shore trips allowed us to visit a number of the many small islands in the Coral Sea, including the Whitsundays and Hamilton and Lizard Islands, famous for their millionaire guests.

Especially fascinating was tying up at the Cooktown jetty and seeing the exact place where Captain Cook's ship, the Endeavour, was beached after being holed by the hidden reef. We climbed the hill where Cook had stood and surveyed the uninhabited surroundings. Looking at the unbroken wilderness stretching to the horizon enabled us to fully appreciate the predicament he found himself in. If he had not managed to repair his ship and navigate it away from the treacherous reefs, the history of Australia would have been completely different.

Cruising the Coral Sea another thought occurred to us: why not stay on a tropical island? Many offer high-class accommodation and have extensive recreational facilities for those who are not satisfied with what nature alone offers. That wasn't for us though. Eventually we found what we wanted.

Heron Island is about 60 miles out from Gladstone and a two-and-a-half-hour trip by fast boat. There are no herons on the island; that was a case of mistaken identity by early explorers. What they saw were egrets. It is a true coral cay and home to thousands of noddy terns and mutton birds which roost there. The birds are so numerous and indifferent to humans that you have to step over them as you walk along the tracks. The island is small enough (just 42 acres) to stroll around the shoreline in less than an hour. It offers comfortable accommodation in the form of separate cabins and a large airy restaurant providing food of a high standard. There is no TV or other entertainment. Your mobile phone will not work here either (good!), so if you want to make a call you have to use the payphone outside the office. What you can do is stroll along the shore and be amazed by the abundant rays, small sharks and solitary turtles a few feet away from you in the clear water. It is perfectly safe to enter the water and swim with them. The fish will simply move away as you approach. There is the so-called Shark Bay which is popular with swimmers, but it is home only to small non-dangerous reef sharks and a species of ray that looks like a shark. When the tide is out a huge expanse of coral is exposed which can be investigated on foot. For these guided, supervised reef walks, you need to don special reef-walking shoes so that you can explore right to the outer edge of the reef, with minimal damage to the coral.

Underwater and underground, Australia offers wonderful experiences in both settings. The lure for me to venture underground was opals. I have always been fascinated by the stone because their random and complex patterns mean no two are alike. Australia produces over 95 per cent of the world's supply of opals and it is the country's national gemstone. In the shopping arcades of the main Australian cities I had admired blazing colours which I had never seen before. Talking to the shop assistants in Brisbane, they told me that the rare and highly prized black and boulder opals were mined at Lightning Ridge. This was a small township just across the border in New South Wales. We could reach it in a couple of days driving so we planned our route and headed south west.

Most Australians live on the coastal rim where all the main cities are located. For me, this journey would be the farthest inland so far. Once we got over the Great Dividing Range we passed through mixed farming country, and around Goondiwindi, where we stopped for the night, we passed cotton fields. We thought cotton growing, which requires a lot of irrigation, was perhaps not a great idea in a country that experiences serious droughts every few years. Continuing west we entered cattle country. The roads we drove on were usually empty of other traffic for mile after mile. But when you come across a herd of several hundred cattle wandering across the highway, accompanied by mounted stockmen, you just have to stop, switch off the engine and enjoy the spectacle. This was bush country – sparse and dry. It was not yet the outback, but it gave me a sense of the immensity of the country.

On our first visit to Lightning Ridge it had the feel of the sort of town you see in classic Western movies. Just two dusty main streets, crossing at right angles lined with basic shops and services – and some impressive opal shops. As we booked into one of the town's two motels we were not anticipating much comfort. But we were wrong. That evening we dined in the motel's restaurant and were impressed by the quality of the food that the kitchen produced.

Every Australian town and city suburb has a social club. Often it is run by the RSL (Returned and Services League of Australia) and they provide bars, restaurants, an entertainment area, sometimes an outdoor bowling green – but always ranks of pokies. (There I go again; pokies are one-armed bandit gambling machines, like in the casinos of Las Vegas.) Australians love to gamble and it has become a serious social problem. But slap bang in the middle of Lightning Ridge was an RSL club with all the usual facilities. Temporary guest membership is quickly provided and we made the most of it during our stay. The town has a large public swimming pool and even a medieval castle, built by a miner who was happy to show us around.

Scattered around the town are the opal mines. These are just compounds marked out on the surface with posts and barbed wire enclosing rusty equipment and piles of mine waste (opal dirt). Not attractive, but this is serious business. Visitors are usually allowed to fossick on the waste and occasionally they find a bit of colour that the miner missed. The more commercially minded owners have a shop above the mine to display their wares and the larger ones provided stairs to allow sightseers safe access into the mine itself. This was the case with the Big Opal, where I made friends with the owner, Lesley. She was a larger-than-life character in all senses and later moved further out to Glengarry where the seams of opal were more productive. Always the businesswoman, she opened a rudimentary bar with basic backpacker accommodation which gloried in the name of The Glengarry Hilton.

The miners at Glengarry were even more feral then the ones on the Ridge and some could have been prototypes for Crocodile Dundee in evolutionary terms. One of Lesley's miner friends invited us to pay a visit to his new mine. The vertically bored shaft was less than three feet in diameter with a flimsy ladder disappearing into the gloom. 'No worries mate' is the standard response to any concerns about health and safety, so I clambered down 30 feet to the working level. In Lesley's workshop we had seen how the raw opal is transformed into the beautiful polished jewel and now crouching and seeing it glistening on the mine walls was entrancing. It was easy to see how people are beguiled with the vision of getting rich quick. For many it becomes a passion and an obsession and they hang on, hoping that next year, the next shaft will bring them their fortune. It doesn't cost much to live out there. Just a basic shack, a dunny out back and a ute with the obligatory dog on the back to get supplies. As much as I love opals, I resisted the temptation.

The sunsets we saw in Australia were fantastic. Vast red canopies... One night we ventured out of town to get away from the electric lights and stopped to gaze at the night sky. The absolute blackness revealed the numerous stars which we only get a hint of in the city.

I celebrated my 65th birthday in style while we were staying at Annette's holiday apartment in Caloundra. Each day our eyes had been drawn to the sky by the drone of a small plane that flew over and left a trail of small dots in its wake. Sky divers! I determined that's what I would like to do to make my day extra special. George enthusiastically agreed and we went to the local airstrip to make the booking. We decided to pay for the optional extra – a video of the whole thing. Otherwise who would believe I had done it? We would each be doing a tandem skydive with an experienced instructor. On the appointed day we met with our dive buddies and they went through the safety checks. My instructor was a tall, charming Czech who wore a white floppy hat that managed to stay on his head without any apparent attachment. Rumour had it that it was nailed on!

Our small plane had a couple of experienced solo divers and four of us dive virgins on board. As the plane climbed to 12,500 feet we had a wonderful view of the hinterland with the Glasshouse Mountains to the west and the glistening sea stretching to the eastern horizon. The weather was perfect; warm and calm with just enough puffy white clouds to give scale to the panorama. Below us we could see the landing spot on a strip of beach we knew well. Two orange beach towels had been laid out crossways to make the target visible. During the plane's ascent we were secured very (very!) firmly to our respective buddies and we were told the drill once again. On leaving the plane we had to lean backwards with our arms folded across our chest. At the chosen altitude the experienced duo went first, then the camera man, who had a small video device fixed firmly to his helmet. He went through the open door and then clung, limpet like, to the outside of the plane so that he could film my exit. The camera was ready; I was ready. Action! They wouldn't be calling 'Cut' and 'Take two' this time!

The dive was fabulous. Because of the height we had reached, we were able to free-fall – probably no more than a minute – before the parachute was deployed. The finished video shows my cheeks rippling with the force of the wind as we plunged earthwards. Well, seawards actually. Once the parachute had opened, it checked our speed and there was the most amazing calm.

The plane had disappeared and there was nothing else up there to make a noise. Absolute silence. It was bliss. I was not aware of the cameraman as he manoeuvred around the sky, but he got to the ground before us so that he could film our approach. The landing was spot perfect and as gentle as a butterfly landing on a flower. It was the most fabulous, never-to-be-forgotten experience. The video shows me grinning and laughing the whole time.

Despite the perception of danger, skydiving is safe and injuries and fatalities are very rare. On the other hand, ping-pong... Now that's another matter!

On our second trip to Heron Island in 2007 calamity struck. It was 25th October and our 39th wedding anniversary. We decided to have a game of table-tennis before going coral viewing. The table was situated under an outside awning and the metal supporting frame was much too close. I stepped back to make my shot and CRACK ...! I was in unbearable pain and could not walk.

The island has a nurse to deal with minor things like sunburn, cuts and coral grazes, but nothing more serious. The nearest hospital was on the mainland and the once-a-day ferry had already departed. The only other alternative was the helicopter that more affluent guests took to reach the island. It would be making a return flight before nightfall. I was given copious amounts of painkiller before I was carefully squeezed into the small, six-seater cabin. We would have preferred to make the scenic helicopter ride over the sea when we could appreciate it properly, but we were relieved to be landing at Gladstone 30 minutes later.

On arrival at the airport an ambulance was waiting to take me straight to the local hospital. It was late evening by the time I was examined by a doctor. She confirmed a suspected fracture, but they could not deal with it at Gladstone. We had to go to Rockhampton, 90 miles away and a good two-hour drive along the Bruce Highway. Major problem; our hire car was parked in the lock-up down at the harbour, but the key was in our cabin on the island, along with all our luggage. This was getting worse and worse. Our adventure was becoming a nightmare.

There was no ambulance service to take us to Rockhampton, so we had to stay the night in Gladstone and make our own transfer arrangements the next day. After I was fitted with a leg splint and given some painkillers I was discharged. We took a taxi to the local motel we had used a few days previously and I spent an uncomfortable night trying to keep my swelling leg in a comfortable position. After an early breakfast George walked into town and hired a second car to transport me to Rockhampton.

The drive to Rockhampton Hospital was uncomfortable and exhausting and we then had to wait a long time in the Accident Department before I was re-examined. An X-ray showed that I had broken a bone just below the knee and I would need an immediate operation. The decision that I needed surgery was a blow to both of us. We had naively assumed that setting my leg in plaster would do the trick. We were so far away from home. When we got over the shock of my needing surgery George dealt with the practicalities. Sensibly, he telephoned our travel insurance company to explain our circumstances. He stayed with me until I was admitted, then headed south back to Gladstone. It was now dark and driving on Australia's narrow country roads at night is risky. Apart from the abundance of wildlife which ventures onto the roads after dusk, there are the huge trucks which thunder along and expect the right of way. They sit on your tail with lights blazing. George could not wait until morning. He had to get back down to Gladstone in time to return the temporary hire car, before getting the morning ferry over to Heron Island and picking up all our belongings. The island staff were aware of our situation and would pack our bags and have them ready at the jetty for the return journey. This was because the boat would only stop long enough to drop off incoming guests and pick up the ones leaving. Urgency was the key word.

Having arrived back at Gladstone Harbour with all our belongings from the island, George retrieved the original hire car and set off north again. At least now he would be travelling in daylight.

By the time George saw me again I had been operated on by a German surgeon, Dr Hohmann. He had repaired the fracture with a metal plate and now I needed rest and somewhere to recover. The hospital was keen to discharge me after five days, but unfortunately, infection had set in and I stayed there for two weeks. George booked himself into a nearby motel and visited me every day with extra treats. He spent time in the motel swimming pool from where he could see the hilltop hospital. In preparation for my release, he purchased a splint and hired a walking frame from the Red Cross which would assist me in hobbling around. The hospital gave George a crash course in post-op care as he would have to give me Clexane anti-clotting injections for the next four weeks, to prevent the dreaded Deep Vein Thrombosis (DVT).

It was a relief to be out of hospital and so before heading south George took me to the nearby Rockhampton Botanic Gardens, so that I could have some immediate respite. There we had an al fresco breakfast under the shade of a giant banyan fig tree accompanied by colourful cheeky parakeets and other native birds who were eager to share our plates. Reinvigorated, we then set off on the long tedious car journey back to Brisbane. There I was restricted to wheelchair outings until our scheduled departure to London two weeks later.

We did not want the disaster to ruin our memory of Heron Island and so we went back for another visit in 2009. Amazingly, despite our complaint about the unsafe table tennis area, nothing had changed. They hadn't even erected a warning notice. On the other hand, this time I was privileged to witness another of nature's great events. At night I watched as green-back turtles hauled their way slowly up the beach to lay their eggs above the high-water mark. Fabulous!

CHAPTER 20
ARTISTS INC. AND MORE

Having combined my various Australian trips into Chapter 19, I hope the reader will realise that some of the events I now relate are not in chronological order.

After we got back to London in 1984 the trip to Oz stayed in my memory. George had kept it from me during our holiday, but on the way back he said he thought he had a hernia and would have to see the doctor when he got home. Well, he did and the upshot was that then he had to go into hospital for an operation to have it repaired. He recovered well and life continued much as it had before, with me working in the press gallery and going to see Mum in Mallorca from time to time. She also came over to visit us in London.

In March 1989 Mum celebrated her 80th birthday with a big party at the West London Synagogue. In the morning Rabbi John Rayner, a colleague of Dad's and a good friend, came over and gave Mum her present. Kerry and Darrell were here for her and she opened all her presents from us and other friends. In the evening we had tables laid out in the Synagogue Council room and she sat under the photograph of Dad and the *Jewish Chronicle* photographer took pictures of all of us. Darrell gave a lovely speech and we all toasted Mum. The atmosphere was warm and welcoming and Mum was very happy. Everything went off beautifully and we took her back to the hotel and then, over a cup of tea, opened the presents our guests had brought her. A few days later Kerry, Mum and I took a lovely break in the Lake District, relaxing and generally chilling out. Mum continued to come over to see us until the journey from Mallorca became too much for her.

In January of that year some of us in the press gallery were invited by the British-Israel Public Affairs Committee (BIPAC) to visit Israel on a fact-finding mission. BIPAC was a Zionist lobby group. It was active from about 1983 to late 1999 when it closed due to lack of funds. Zelda Harris escorted journalists to and during the trip to Israel. She invited political journalists from the press gallery, including the political editor of *The Times*. The schedule was such that we were busy seeing people and visiting historic sites all day long. It was a hectic few days and by the end of the visit we all needed a recovery holiday!

I knew we would be seeing the Speaker of the Israeli Parliament, the Knesset, so had asked the current Speaker of the House of Commons, Bernard Weatherill to give me a letter of introduction. Bernard was a charming man and later he wrote the foreword to my book of poems called *MPs in Verse*.

We went to the Knesset on the first day and I was able to deliver the letter. We met some of the MKs – the Members of the Knesset. We met a couple who were involved in trying to get Arab and Jewish clerics together. There were many secret projects of this kind taking place then, and for all I know it is still going on today between people who want to see some positive action to facilitate a peaceful outcome to the Arab-Israeli struggle.

We were privileged to see places that were not on the tourist map and one of those was the West Bank. We saw the Brigadier General, Shaika Erezat at his headquarters in Beit El. We saw an Arab refugee camp and I wondered why the refugees couldn't be given proper housing with all the Arab money the oil was bringing in. We also saw the Jewish settlements and I again wondered why they had to be extended when they provoked such anger and resentment amongst the Arabs.

An interesting visit took place when we went to the Druze village of Yirka. We were allowed to spend time with the host Sallah Sallah and his wife and 10 children who played around us. They were a delightful family. I had never come across the Druze people before but really took to them.

We travelled across beautiful countryside and went past Tiberius to a kibbutz on the Lebanese border. There was a fence on the right-hand side of the road and that made me feel uneasy. On the Friday we drove to the Golan Heights and crossed the River Jordan. I found this whole trip to Israel unreal. Seeing the road signs to places I had only read about in the Bible was weird. So it was with that feeling that I joined our group in Jerusalem for our ride to Masada. It took a long time to get there, as on the way we passed all sorts of fascinating places. En route we saw the Church of Ascension of Jesus 40 days after his resurrection. We gazed at Bedouin tents and Bedouins out tending their flock. Some of them were riding donkeys. We stopped at

Jericho and saw the excavations of the walls. From a compound Bedouins were offering touristic items and trinkets for sale and I bought a necklace from them.

On the last lap to Masada we passed the caves where the Dead Sea Scrolls had been found. We finally made it to Masada. It was quite difficult getting to the top, but when we did it was incredible to ponder that here the Jews committed suicide rather than surrender to the Romans. From the top of the mountain which sits 1300 feet above the Red Sea, we had the most incredible view of the Judean desert and Jordan. It supposedly hardly ever rains on Masada, but suddenly while we were on top of the mountain, the heavens opened and rain gushed down the mountain in several waterfalls. People who were taking pictures of the remains of the elaborate buildings, stopped and began to photograph the downpour. It didn't last long and we then made our way back down again. The next treat awaited – swimming in the Dead Sea. I managed to have a photo taken reading a paper whilst lying down in the salty water.

That was a great climax to our visit and I have never forgotten it.

* * * *

Life continued in the press gallery where I had been interviewing our regional MPs for years. For a while now it had occurred to me that I could contribute something positive by becoming a Member of Parliament myself.

In 1990 I approached the appropriate party office regarding my ambition and eventually was invited to spend a weekend away to learn what was required of a prospective parliamentary candidate. We were scrutinised by anonymous observers all the time, even during meals. We took part in debates and I found this easy as I had done it all before at the end of my Bar finals.

Having been approved as suitable material at the end of the two days, I then had the task of going for interviews up and down the country with the prospect of fighting a by-election. It would be a constituency where there was no hope of my winning it, but was a challenge just to see how I performed. I went to several interviews, but I always seemed to miss out on being picked. On one occasion I was asked if I would be prepared to fight the next election on an aggressive and personal basis. This implied attacking my opponent's character. When I told them I would only fight on political issues, they signalled that this was the end of my chance to be their candidate at the next election. After a few similar experiences I became quite disillusioned and gave up any idea of entering politics.

George and I were still living in the house in Hendon, which to be honest was now too big for just the two of us. By 1990 both Kerry and Darrell had left home and we had room to spare. They both came around regularly though and we all enjoyed playing snooker on the eight-by-four table we had jointly funded.

We didn't want to move into another house as we thought with the passing years, going up and down stairs and the upkeep of a garden might be difficult. Consequently, we decided to look for a flat.

We looked round the neighbouring areas to see what was on offer. A new block had just been built in Whetstone and there were still one or two flats to be sold, so we had a look at them. The view from the rear balconies was over allotments and beyond that we could see and enjoy the green belt. The rooms were large with high ceilings and we liked what we saw. The flats were on the main High Road so we could walk to the shops, dentist and doctor's surgery. The buses passed the front door and the London Underground station was a short walk away. All very convenient. We put in an offer and it was accepted. We moved in during 1991 and have been here ever since.

In the mid '90s, I finished working in the House of Commons and became a consultant with Burson-Marsteller, the well-known public relations company. When that contract ended, I decided to put together an amateur drama group. It took me a year or so to find the right people and get everyone together but finally we were all assembled. We called ourselves 'STARS Theatre Company' and in 1997, we went up to the Edinburgh Fringe with Lorca's *Blood Wedding*. I played the mother and the play was well received. We had excellent reviews in the local newspaper. Unfortunately after that, some members thought they could run the show better than I could and so I left it to them. The company lasted a little while longer, but then disintegrated. All my hard work gone by the board. Oh well – on to other things...

From an early age I have loved to paint. Maybe it was in my genes from my grandmother's uncle, the famous artist Hermann Struck, but whenever I had the chance, I would put paintbrush to paper. I adore putting colours together and am known for my vivid sunsets and flowers. I decided to enter an art competition that Barnet Hospital was running, where the best painting would be displayed on the ward walls. I won it and thereafter, several of my paintings were displayed in the hospital. I hope they cheered up the patients. The organisers of the competition suggested I spend a year at Barnet College, doing an art course as this might help me to show my work. I agreed and enjoyed the discipline of working to a timetable. It is difficult to persuade art galleries to exhibit your work, so I came to the conclusion that it would be good to have my own.

How to fulfil that ambition... it would need start-up capital but, as usual, we did not have any spare money.

George then became my knight in shining armour. Through retraining, he had transferred his skills from engineering and building design to writing computer software. His inventiveness and his ability to think outside the box, combined with the discipline of precision learnt at the drawing board, made him an excellent analyst and programmer. I introduced him to Geoff Bradley, a member of my synagogue, who created the Mencap Business Supplies Company. George was an invaluable help to him.

Later George formed his own software company which did a lot of consultancy work for major companies and was in great demand. When Kerry set up her own recruitment business he designed a bespoke system for her business which enabled all the consultants to work in the most productive and efficient way.

He received a commission to develop an application for one of London's leading photo agencies. By photo agency I mean the *paparazzi* who take the exclusive celebrity photos that end up in our newspapers, magazines and on TV. Apparently the revenue splits when photographic reproduction rights are sold can become complex. There was no suitable product on the market, so George took on the difficult challenge and devised a solution that handled the task with ease. The head of a major California-based agency congratulated George by saying "... you have solved the very specific problems of photo agency billing which I have not seen in any other software. Well done!"

With the profits from that assignment George generously said he would finance the gallery, so the next step was to find suitable premises. We found a suite of first-floor rooms above a local gas showroom, decided they would serve our requirements and signed a lease. There was a lot to do by way of refurbishment. The worst surprise was lifting the ceiling hatch only to discover that the roof space was filled with hundreds of roosting pigeons. Up to that time it had never occurred to me that I had never ever seen a baby pigeon. Well I had now! The scene was quite pitiful. Because of the health hazard we had to have the space professionally cleared and fumigated After that we installed appropriate wall fittings, spot lighting, a security system, furniture and the 101 other things we hadn't thought of before. We also had to take out suitable insurance to cover the paintings and other valuable art objects which would be on display.

I called my gallery Artists Inc. (ink, get it?) and we had a grand opening in February 2000. There was a good mix of talented artists' work on display and the major name was our local Barnet-based sculptor, John Somerville. He is famous for his statues of pop legends such as John Lennon, Jimi Hendrix and Mick Jagger and small-scale versions of these were on sale. He casts his work in various materials including silver, bronze, and resin. I loved his range of humorous candles based on political figures of the '70s and '80s and I still have a full set, unconsumed by fire.

We did sell some paintings but business wasn't good. It probably didn't help that the entrance was via the service road at the back of the shops and there were flights of external and internal stairs to climb. We were losing money but the decider was when the landlord's son, who came swaggering in occasionally to see how we were getting on, took a swing at George in the street. The son was known to the police in connection with drug offences and we decided that we wouldn't risk the gallery becoming associated with activities and aggression of that sort. We closed just five months later in July. Although the gallery did not do well, I did get a return on our efforts. I made two valuable friendships from the artists who exhibited with us – Carol Baker and Rosemary Anthony, who have remained close friends ever since.

To celebrate Mum's 96th birthday on 27th March 2005, I went over to Mallorca with Rosemary and her husband, Keeling. Mum was very frail and by the end of the visit, I had the feeling she did not have long to live. I was scheduled to go to Kerch in the Ukraine on 6th April for five days to visit our sister congregation. I was in two minds whether to go as I did not want to be so far away from home if Mum passed before I got back. In the end I decided to take a chance. I think someone was looking out for me, because I got back from Kerch on the Monday and Mum actually passed on just two days later.

It was so sad to see my once beautiful, vibrant and full of life mother deteriorate into an unrecognisable stranger. She was generous and full of love, but had her faults as we all have. She never did understand George's dry sense of humour, but I put that down to her lack of English. More significantly, she put her trust in the wrong people, and didn't trust me as she should have done. I have never understood why this was. I have never wanted anything more than to help her, especially as she got older, but she thought I was not trustworthy to look after her. Instead, Kerry took on the burden and did a fantastic job of sorting out her affairs. When she died, we both ran around arranging everything for her body to come back to London. That took a few days and she was buried in the same grave as my father.

CHAPTER 21
GRANDMOTHER'S PAIN

By 2011, I was a grandmother to two children, but I did not have access to them. I am not alone in this predicament and it is a problem and a hardship for many grandparents. There is wide public concern regarding this common situation and it is regularly discussed in the media. Grandparents have no automatic rights to see their grandchildren. Governments frequently make pronouncements on changing the law and in 2010 both David Cameron and Nick Clegg gave speeches on the subject. In 2010, the *Daily Telegraph* ran a story under the headline 'increased legal rights for grandparents under new family reform'. A review of the family justice system is now underway to consider how the system can best provide greater contact rights for grandparents, but as yet there has been no change.

My children, Kerry and Darrell, had a close and rewarding relationship with their grandparents and I hoped my grandchildren would have the same with me.

For years I have had no contact with my two granddaughters, who were, by 2011, seven and five. I was not even told when their baby blessing took place in the synagogue. A friend called to congratulate me on the event and that was the first I had heard of it. I was faced with the unenviable choice of either not seeing my grandchildren, or having to resort to legal process to try to have contact. This time it would be in the Family Division of my local county court. How had this unnecessary and tragic situation come about?

When my son Darrell was in his mid-thirties he met the woman who would later become his wife. Up to then he had been a part of our normal family life. He, with his sister Kerry, would regularly visit us in our home and we helped and advised them when they wanted to get on the property ladder. George had been a wonderful stepfather and assisted Darrell with his homework, introduced him to computers, passed on his DIY practical skills, played badminton with him and later taught him to windsurf. He did all the countless things that any good dad would do. We went on holidays together and went down to Mudeford with our motor van to enjoy windsurfing in Christchurch Harbour. On the occasions of my mother's birthdays we always found a nice upmarket restaurant in which to celebrate. Once we all stayed at the famous Swan Hotel in the old timbered village of Lavenham, in the lovely Suffolk countryside.

So, our life with Darrell was a normal affectionate one and when Darrell was ready to continue his studies after leaving school, we helped him find a place at Liverpool University. We drove him up there in October 1980, settling him in to his campus digs. We hoped he would find his feet and do well in his studies. However, he failed his first-year examinations and was told he could not retake them. We were disappointed to say the least when he arrived at our front door, dishevelled. We told him it was time for him to leave the nest and stand on his own two feet as he was now twenty years old.

Not long afterwards we invited Darrell to travel with us to Switzerland and we had a good holiday there. He frequently came over to see us in our Hendon home, for which he retained a door key, and we remained a loving family unit.

Then he met his future wife, Marie and they got engaged. Instead of bringing her over for coffee informally, so that we could get to know her, the first time we met her as a family was when we invited her with Darrell and Kerry to our Passover meal. She behaved in a cool and unfriendly manner and seemed oblivious to the efforts we were making to welcome her into our family. George likes to chat and joke and have fun with people and has a dry sense of humour, but on this occasion it fell on stony ground. It was not an auspicious beginning.

She is a solicitor. She had previously been married and divorced. From the start it seemed she had decided that she wanted nothing to do with George. Marie told Kerry at that time that she was not prepared to have a family relationship with George, but would with me. She gave no reason for this then, and it was not until the court case started that the issue was raised by my son and Marie. Apparently, Darrell had told her that George had treated him badly as a child. Our refuting of this falsehood would become part of our evidence in the later legal proceedings.

So, there were strained relationships leading up to the wedding in April 1998. It also did not help that sometime before the wedding, Darrell phoned me in distress and confided that Marie was telling him he must choose between me and her. This must have been a terrible dilemma for him.

Darrell had been living on his own for many years and had never tried to regain contact with his natural father during this time. Now, suddenly, he and Marie had started to see him.

I was not looking forward to the wedding day as it was made clear to me that I was to have nothing to do with any of the arrangements and I was only to invite four people. The actual ceremony took place at West London Synagogue and the officiating rabbi was Charles Emmanuel, then the rabbi at Alyth. During the wedding ceremony, no mention was made of my father who had served at both synagogues. After the synagogue service, when groups were being assembled for photographs, George, Kerry and I were not included. I felt unwelcome and abandoned by my son. George decided not to attend the reception as he felt he would be blamed for anything that might go wrong.

The wedding reception took place at the Café Royal in the West End of London. Darrell and Marie had around two hundred guests, but I just had my permitted four friends. Before we sat down I met Marie's mother and we managed to chat together amicably alone. She told me that Marie had forbidden her to talk to me and if she knew she had done so, there would be trouble.

The MC announced the groups that were to be assembled for photographs, first the bride's family and then various others such as the drama group to which Darrell belonged. I and my daughter were not included in any of them. Eventually, the MC announced that anyone who had not yet been called could go downstairs and have their photo taken. Kerry and I were the only two who had not been mentioned, so we went downstairs where the photographer was waiting. The bride was absent and did not have her photo taken with us.

The wedding reception was a nightmare for me and Kerry. I was placed at the far end of the top table, away from my son, and my daughter was at a table some distance from me. In his speech Darrell did not mention me or my family. Rabbi Emmanuel told me he had been asked by people at his table, whether the bridegroom's mother was dead. Darrell was profuse in his praise for his wife's family and failed to make any mention of my family, especially my mother who was extremely generous to him.

I was very upset but thought that if I was to have any kind of relationship with my son and his wife in the future, I had better do something about it. Towards the end of the reception I approached Marie and suggested we should start again. Sadly, she rejected the hand of friendship and arrogantly pointed out that the two hundred wedding guests were her friends. The indication to me, was that she had no further use for me. I came away from her in tears and Darrell saw me. I don't know if he was sorry for what had happened, but he took me in his arms and said, "Mum, I know it is not your fault" and kissed me.

I still cannot understand why I was treated in this manner.

After the wedding, my mother (who was still living in Mallorca) persuaded Marie to phone me. Marie did, but used the opportunity to wrongly accuse me of saying bad things about her to her colleagues' wives at the reception. This was totally untrue and contrary to my nature, but in any event I did not know the colleagues, never mind their wives. The horror of their wedding day and reception will remain with me for the rest of my life.

Family relationships deteriorated rapidly after the wedding. I no longer saw Darrell or received birthday or Mother's Day cards from him and I miss his affection.

It was only some years later that we discovered that Marie had been looking into my mother's private financial affairs, even before she married my son. After my father died in 1984 my mother wanted to stay living in the apartment in El Arenal. As she got older and increasingly infirm she needed home care help and this was provided and arranged solely by Kerry and myself.

In 2003, Kerry and I had been on one of our regular visits to see my mother in Mallorca. We arrived at her apartment to be told by her carer that Marie had just rushed down the stairs when she heard the lift arriving, realising it was us. We were amazed that she was there at all. My mother, who was over 90 years old, should not have been disturbed without prior consultation with Kerry or me. It became clear why Marie departed in such a hurry, as we found my mother in a terribly distressed state. It turned out that Marie had been upsetting my mother because of the power-of-attorney she had granted Kerry a long time before.

I felt bewildered and hurt that Darrell would allow Marie's visits to my mother to take place without my or Kerry's knowledge. She had never sought permission from either of us to look into my mother's private financial affairs. Darrell and Marie should have been completely open with us about what she was doing.

I decided to resume contact with my son and Marie a few years after the wedding, and I went round to see them without telling George. This was because he was upset on my account at what had happened in the past and was fearful of me being hurt again. After my first granddaughter was born, I had sporadic contact with her until the last time I saw her, which was when she was two years old. A very nasty incident had confirmed George's fears and I realised deceiving him was foolish and could even damage my relationship with him.

Darrell and Marie now have two daughters and, at the time of writing, I still have not managed to see them in my own home. Darrell refused to bring them over to me. He wrote and told me that George was not a relative and I must stop him sending cards signed as Grandpa George. When George asked Darrell (via email) to explain how, as his legal stepfather, he wasn't a relative and what suitable alternative title Darrell would prefer him to use, there was no reply.

After five years of not seeing Darrell, I managed to persuade him to meet with me at the nearby Brent Cross Shopping Mall. I again wanted to try and sort matters out between us. He would not agree to me seeing my grandchildren and said I should not mention them again. At that point things reached an impasse. There had been several cases in the papers concerning grandparents being denied access to their grandchildren and then making applications to the family courts for 'contact orders'. I told Darrell that if I were left with no other alternative I would apply for such an order. He said things would get worse if I did that, but I replied that it could not be any worse than it already was.

In March 2011, the *Daily Mail* carried a front-page article with the headline: 'THE RIGHT TO SEE YOUR GRANDCHILD'. It quoted a Minister saying, "it is a scandal there is little or no recognition of the vital role grandparents play in society". The *Grandparent Times*, the newsletter of the respected Grandparents' Association said that in recent years the courts have shown an increasing tendency to grant contact orders in favour of grandparents. That gave me hope that the mood was changing, but I was depressed at the thought of having to go to court again.

George and I began researching online to find out what to do next. We had previous experience of courts, of course, but that was a long time ago and there is little margin for error in cases like this. Navigation through the legal process and ensuring you do everything correctly is essential. We purchased the Legal-Zone Guide on how to make an application in the Family Court, and found it very useful.

I was still extremely reluctant to seek a legal remedy and so before filing the court documents I wrote to Darrell and Marie pleading with them to make arrangements which would render it unnecessary. The response was a letter to me from Darrell which stunned me. In it, for the first time, he made references to a 'traumatised childhood' marked by beatings and psychological abuse. He accused me and George of the most loathsome acts. He even cast aspersions on the excellent voluntary work George did for the Victim Support charity over a period of many years. He said his natural father was a model of decency, loyalty and kindness. We were bewildered by his complete rejection of me and George. The happy childhood he had shared with Kerry spanned 16 years, and she was taken aback by his denial of the reality of that period.

Because of this we felt we had no option but to make an application to the courts. We concentrated on completing the forms C2 and C100 which we filed at the court with the required fee of £200.

In spite of the frequent discussion in the media of the right of grandparents to see their grandchildren, at the time of making the application there was no right enshrined in law. So the first step was to obtain 'leave' to submit an application. It's a convoluted procedure and we ran the risk of failing at that very first hurdle. Applications can get quite complicated and there was a lot we didn't know. Yet we were naively optimistic and decided to proceed with the application as we had nothing to lose. At least, even if we were not to succeed in having contact with the grandchildren, it would be on the record that we had tried everything to see them. No one could tell them that their paternal grandmother and step-grandfather had not wanted to see them. Success in court does not only depend on the law. The allocation of judges to hear cases is random and fortunately we were to have a fair and sympathetic District Judge.

There are some restrictions on the reporting of proceedings in Family Courts, so I will only recount what happened outside the court.

We arrived at the court in good time and sat in the public waiting area with a friend. We were approached by a man in a dark suit who did not introduce himself but just handed us a document. He then turned to leave. George rose and asked him who he was. I thought the man was rude and uncooperative. I eventually discovered that he was the respondent's counsel. In the court precincts it is customary to be respectful of everyone you meet and behave in a dignified manner. The way we were given the document seemed to me to be discourteous.

We were even more astonished when we read through the two-page document he had given us. It was entitled 'Case Summary' and consisted of a list of accusations concerning events going back forty-six years. It repeated and added to the accusations Darrell had made in his letter to me. A case summary should be a neutral outline of the facts and issues, agreed by all parties and presented to the court when requested. This was nothing of the sort; it was an inflammatory character assassination. The respondents' legal team had made no attempt to involve us in the preparation of what should be an impartial, jointly agreed document.

The case summary contained no information as to who prepared it or any contact details. We were appalled by the contents and the way it had been presented to us so that after that hearing, George wrote a letter of rebuke to the counsel.

At the hearing a court welfare officer was present. The judge directed her to meet privately with both sides before proceeding further. This she did and was positive when she spoke to us, especially when George made a generous offer to withdraw from the proceedings. We thought it may help to resolve matters quickly. This was reported back to the judge and we were all recalled into the court room. It was obvious to us that the respondent's counsel hoped to have the case dismissed, but at the end of the brief hearing the judge adjourned the case, granting us leave to restore.

We retired to think about what had happened. We had not got far. We had not been given leave, but on the other hand our application for contact had not been dismissed. Should we throw in the towel or press on? The attempted character assassination from my own son was beyond my understanding. Rather than leave that damaging portrayal of us on the record, in case the court believed it, we felt we had to continue and defend ourselves.

But more importantly, I wanted contact with my grandchildren. So a few weeks later we lodged our application to restore the case. The matter dragged on for a whole year.

At the next hearing, both sides were ordered to prepare statements of their evidence and this gave us the opportunity to deal with all the numerous accusations, distortions and untruths contained in the case summary. This task was distressing for me as I tried to comprehend the untruthful allegations from my son Darrell, whom I had nurtured and loved – and still love. Fortunately, we had support and help from friends in the legal professions. One was Aubrey Rose, a solicitor who knew us as a family and he not only gave us valuable advice, but also wrote a character reference for me.

Rosemarie Buess, the au pair girl who had lived with us when Darrell and Kerry were children, also gave us a glowing reference. We had a fulsome reference from Jane Carmichael, whom we had met when we took up badminton after moving to Hendon. She and her husband, Keith had three lovable small daughters and we, but especially George, delighted in their company and they in his. Jane and Keith had no reservations about us taking their children on a seaside holiday on our own, twice. (This was in 1990 when Darrell was 29.) On the basis of her witnessing these close relationships, Jane, now a probation officer, was able to write an extremely favourable character reference for George. The accusations by my son and daughter-in-law that my grandchildren – or any children – were unsafe in the proximity of me or George were repulsive. We could not let the allegations go uncontested and these testimonies would be important.

I also obtained a testimonial from Sir Sigmund Sternberg. He was the founder of the Sternberg Centre which became the Finchley home of the Leo Baeck College and he founded the Three Faiths Forum and is a well-known philanthropist. We had known each other for many years and served together on the Board of Deputies of British Jews. At the other end of the age scale, George was given an enthusiastic reference from 14-year-old Zack, son of family friends Bim and Ruth, who also supplied a reference. We had looked after Zack on occasion and taken him on outings to museums. He said that we had been like another set of grandparents to him.

My daughter Kerry also prepared a statement, being the only close witness of Darrell's childhood. She was shocked at her brother's untrue recollections regarding their shared past. She has been supportive and loyal to us all through the years and has not seen Darrell since his wedding because of the way he treated us. She is heartbroken at losing her brother.

When we exchanged statements with the other side's solicitors, our bundle of documents included over forty photographs showing evidence of the happy family life we enjoyed with Darrell, Kerry and my parents. In addition, we were able to include extracts from the various independent reports prepared by the High Court welfare officers when Darrell was a child. They confirmed indisputably the safe, secure, contented home life he had shared with Kerry.

Incredibly, in their statements Darrell and Marie had taken the opportunity to not only repeat their horrible allegations, but also to elaborate upon them. Not one iota of evidence was produced to support their increasingly absurd claims. They opposed my application on the grounds that the grandchildren would be put at risk of mental and physical harm if I was allowed contact.

Nobody's childhood is perfect – mine certainly wasn't, and nor was George's, but neither of us blamed our parents and eliminated them from our lives. In Darrell's condemnation of us he did not admit to a single positive feature of his childhood. It was this unrelieved bleak view of his childhood that we could not understand. If there had been personal matters he could not discuss with me, George or his sister, he could have confided in his grandparents or numerous family friends. From our point of view Darrell had a good childhood and didn't appear to have any 'issues' until he met Marie and became reunited with his father.

At the interview before the last hearing for contact, we had been informed by the welfare officer that the grandchildren did not have any knowledge of me at all! In spite of the cards we sent them – and Darrell telling me they had received them – it was now claimed they had never been told about me. If this were true, how would ignorance of my existence help them as they grow up? Children become inquisitive about family history as they mature. What would my granddaughters be told about the illustrious van der Zyl name? I was taken aback that my son could let me believe the children knew about me when he now claimed they did not.

The final hearing was the day before my birthday in April 2012. By then my son and daughter-in-law had dismissed their counsel and solicitor and were appearing in person. Darrell stated in court that he never ever wanted to see me again. He had prepared a written 15-page final submission which did not please the judge because it rehashed all the hostile family history once more. By comparison, my spoken submission was concise and I quoted a fundamental legal principle which Sir George Baker had cited when I marshalled for him in the Baader-Meinhof case many years before. It states that 'no person can take advantage of their own wrong'. I cannot know for sure if the judge was persuaded by it, but no regard was paid to any of the wicked accusations made by the respondents.

At the end of the day, because of the existing family animosity, a contact order was not given. The court considered it would not be in the children's best interests. I was very disappointed, but I remain optimistic that one day my granddaughters, through their own initiative, will find me and learn about the efforts I made to see them. They will then learn about their rich family heritage and the history of the eminent name they bear.

Darrell and Marie had applied for an order that we pay the considerable costs which they had accrued, and I was relieved when it was disallowed.

I hope that by recounting my fight to see my grandchildren it will help the campaign to change the law regarding grandparents' access rights.

We had previously learnt that Darrell was undergoing counselling and I earnestly hope that it will help him. Maybe one day he will be able to acknowledge the loving childhood he enjoyed with us and his sister.

The judge, in her summing up, had advised that there should be no more upsetting correspondence between the parties. But, just a few days after the court case had ended, I received a disturbing letter from Marie's father. We had no prior knowledge of this person, never having had any previous communication with him and he had not been a party to the court case. It was additionally offensive to receive unsolicited letters addressed to 'Mrs Rooker' when, as everyone knows, I use my maiden name for all purposes – even in court. George wrote to Darrell and Marie asking them to intervene and stop the sender harassing us.

That miserable episode of my life is now over and I have more interesting things on the horizon to look forward to.

CHAPTER 22
AFTERTHOUGHTS

Bond-related events keep cropping up in unexpected ways. In 2010, I went along to the BBC's *Antiques Roadshow* when it visited Hatfield House, which is about ten miles from my home. This 400-year-old Jacobean house replaced an earlier building where Queen Elizabeth I spent her childhood. The building and grounds have featured in many films including *Cromwell, Sherlock Holmes, Shakespeare in Love* and *Batman*. I took with me a painting, some jewellery and my copy of the *Goldfinger* screenplay which I used during filming with Gert Fröbe. The show's host, Fiona Bruce, pounced on the screenplay saying she was a great Bond fan and insisted that she interview me for the show. That was fun in itself, but it did not end there.

The show was not broadcast until spring 2011, and afterwards I received an email from Helen who was the personal assistant to a senior executive of a major international company which makes computer networking equipment. She had watched the show and claimed to have had an epiphany! When we spoke to each other on the phone she explained that her Swiss boss was frequently called on to make speeches in English in front of live audiences or via worldwide video links. He was adept in every way except one; his Swiss-German accent and the lilting delivery diminished his presentations. He had already received voice coaching but needed something extra. Helen said that from the work I had done revoicing another famous Swiss (Ursula Andress), she was convinced I would be able to help her boss. Well I wouldn't be revoicing him, but I said I would give it my best shot.

It was quickly arranged for me to be flown over to Zurich to coach the man before his next major speech, two weeks hence. I was put up in a top hotel and next day met up with Herr M. He was utterly charming and we got on well, speaking in both English and German. Apart from my film work, during my years working at the House of Commons I had been involved with tutoring MPs in vocal communication skills and public speaking and so I was able to prepare a package of relevant material. Herr M. rapidly absorbed my suggestions and everyone was highly pleased with the improvements.

Another Bond link came a short time before the end of the court case. I had received, completely out-of-the-blue, a telephone call from Douglas Emery. He was assistant to Taryn Simon, the noted New York-based photographer who is famous for her special projects. Her book *The Innocents* contains photographs and interviews with people who had been exonerated after being wrongly convicted of crimes in the USA. In preparation for her next project she was in Paris finishing a photo-shoot of all the actresses associated with the Bond films. The team had been in London for three weeks, but unaccountably, hadn't been told about my part in the films. Could I come over straight away so that I could be included before they returned home?

I was recovering from a bout of pneumonia at that time and so needed clearance from my physician, Dr Rapti Mediwake at Barnet Hospital. She said it would be OK provided I was accompanied by a carer. So George and I headed off to Paris on the Eurostar. Taryn was pleased with my contribution and it will be included in her photo-installation which, hopefully, will be exhibited in London and Berlin as well as New York and other cities. Paris is my favourite city and so George and I extended our stay there to four days and it made a nice break in the middle of the litigation.

On my last visit to Berlin I had met up with Herr Bernt Roder, the head of the Pankow Museum. This is located in the north of the city and covers the three boroughs of Weissensee, Pankow and Prenzlauer Berg, where I was born. He was interested in my family history and keen to put on an exhibition celebrating and honouring my father's life as a rabbi. It is scheduled for some time in 2013 and will also feature some aspects of my life, as well as displaying some of my art.

In Schwerte, Germany, Dad is honoured by having a plaque displayed on the house where he was born. In addition, there is a campaign to name a street or a square after him. It is good that he is being recognised in Germany after what my family went through. I am also trying to make sure his work in founding the Leo Baeck College in London is properly appreciated. To this end, I have been fundraising with my friend, Pat Hasenson, with whom I grew up at Alyth, plus the current Rabbi Mark Goldsmith. My father's main concern was always the welfare of the young, as they will become the leaders of tomorrow. We have received donations from people my father helped when they were young. This is why the money will be used to help the next generation of rabbis at the college.

My life has been full of twists and turns; it's certainly been full of surprises and I have met many fascinating people along the way. I didn't plan it – and sometimes I cannot believe I had the time to do it all – but somehow I managed to become successful in three demanding professions. I was a paid-up member of Actors Equity, later I was admitted to Middle Temple as a barrister and lastly I joined the National Union of Journalists. Officially I am retired, but I keep busy writing poetry, painting (mostly flowers and sunsets) and giving concerts and talks about my various careers. Most recently, I discovered I had a gift for healing and undertook a course with the Healing Trust whereby I now give hands-on healing once a week.

George and I have adopted the term *pensioneer* – created by the incorrect pronunciation of 'pensioner' by *Star Trek's* William Shatner on a recent TV news quiz. I like to think that nothing can stop we *pensioneers* from boldly going on to new challenges.

I have been fortunate to have had the opportunity to travel to many beautiful places with George. We have seen Niagara Falls and the Taj Mahal. We have been on cruises along the Nile and the Rhine. We try to spend a lot of time in Switzerland, the birthplace of George's mother. In recent years many of my German Bond fans have become genuinely close friends. They are all of a younger generation and I have enjoyed their generous invitations to visit and stay with them in their homes. Knowing Olly, Markus, Wolfgang and Carsten has allowed me to feel perfectly at ease in modern-day Germany.

On a visit to the USA I visited the synagogue in Santa Monica, California where Dad had been offered a pulpit after he fled Germany. Who can tell how my life would have turned out had he taken up that offer? I would have been living close to the epicentre of the film world, so anything could have happened. But I have no complaints. Que sera, sera.

* * * * *

George and me with our motor van.

My 60th birthday with Kerry, George and Darrell

My 65th birthday sky dive

The plaque reads:

Historische Schwerter Persönlichkeit:

**Oberrabbiner
Dr. Werner van der Zyl**
1902 – 1984

Geburtshaus

Mitbegründer des Jüdischen Theologischen
Colleges in London; verhalf während der
nationalsozialistischen Verfolgung zahlreichen
jüdischen Jugendgruppen zur Flucht.

The commemorative plaque to Dad in Schwerte

Bubble bath in Lucerne

40th Wedding Anniversary in Frankfurt with German Bond fans, 2008

With Fiona Bruce at the BBC Antiques Roadshow, 2010

With Roger Moore at his book launch 2008

POSTSCRIPT

At the time of writing this book in 2012, it is the 50th anniversary of the first Bond movie. As I began this autobiography reminiscing about my part in the making of *Dr. No* it is perhaps fitting that I end with some movie-related comments.

Apart from those I have discussed in this book, I contributed to over 90 other films. These include *Battle of Britain, Fiddler on the Roof, Scars of Dracula* (Jenny Handley), *The Cherry Picker* (Lulu), *The Quiller Memorandum, Robin Hood* and *Z*.

I also voiced commercials for such companies as Avon, Boots, British Airways, Cadbury's, Max Factor and Watneys and also contributed to several TV series. A full list can be found on my website.

The 24 Bond movies produced by EON are the second highest-grossing film series ever after *Harry Potter*, based on box office receipts. However, when adjusted for inflation, the Bond films have the highest grossing profits of all time.

When the filming on set or on location ends, a movie is not finished. The meticulous process called post-production then begins. The film goes to the editing suite where music and sound effects are added and unwanted scenes are removed. It's not uncommon for lots of footage to end up on the cutting-room floor. Some people think post-production is the most important and creative part of movie making and it can certainly help to make or break a film.

Revoicing is both art and artifice combined. It is skilful deception which can repair defects and improve performances. It is a bit like fine-tuning a car while still on the production line. The Bond films were finessed to perfection. Would they have succeeded without fine actors in the leading roles, or minus the memorable, catchy 007 theme music or with heroines speaking in dodgy accents? I don't think so and I am proud to have been part of the combined effort that contributed to making such great movies.

Movie making is about creating illusions. Make-up is used to hide flaws, enhance features and add character. Some stars insist on being filmed from their 'best' side only. Diminutive stars have been known to stand on boxes (Alan Ladd) or wear elevator shoes (Sylvester Stallone) to make them seem taller. We know people don't really get injured or killed in films, no matter how extreme the action looks. With special effects and today's astonishing computer wizardry, anything can be made to seem genuine. In short, all moviegoers know that what they are watching is make-believe.

I adored Audrey Hepburn, but it does not diminish my appreciation of her to know that it was not her voice singing in *My Fair Lady* but that of Marni Nixon. Even my sound studio colleague Tony Curtis was revoiced in *Some Like It Hot*. He couldn't quite manage an acceptable falsetto voice for his drag character Josephine, so American artist Paul Frees was called in to supply the goods. Amazingly Frees had also revoiced lines for many other stars including Humphrey Bogart, Orson Welles, Kirk Douglas, Peter Lorre and Bela Lugosi.

Apart from Lois Maxwell who played Miss Moneypenny in the Bond movies, I was involved with more Bond films than any other actress. Yet it has always remained a mystery to me why my work in revoicing numerous actresses was not officially recognised. As a partner in the successful, collaborative endeavour which the Bond films are, it seems strange that my name has never appeared on the screen.

* * * *

Astonishingly, even at the time of completing the final chapter of this book, efforts are being made to deny me my place in movie history. In April 2012 I was invited to be a special guest at the Goldfinger Day film convention to be held in September in London. Because I was on set throughout the shooting of *Goldfinger* they said I had a fascinating experience to share and Bond fans would love to meet me.

Two months later the invitation was withdrawn. The reason, as I was told, was because of objections being made by one of the actresses I had revoiced in the Bond films. It was always the directors and producers who decided which characters needed to be revoiced. There was nothing personal about it on my part. I just did my professional job after the shooting had ended. I was looking forward to the launch of my book at the celebratory occasion and was devastated when my invitation was cancelled.

Two days after the events described above, my name was also removed from the official website that sells Bond merchandise. No prior warning or explanation was given.

In spite of my significant contribution to the early success of the Bond phenomenon I have not been invited to any of the 50th jubilee year celebrations being held at Pinewood or elsewhere.

Is the truth about the part I played in creating the Bond Girls' image really so damaging?

THE END

Photograph Glamour mode 3 was taken by Christopher Thynne.
All the others were taken by me, or are owned by me or members of my family.

Visit my website for more information and photos.

Connect with Me Online: www.nikkivanderzyl.co.uk

INDEX

H

I

J

M

N

O

P

Q

R